2024 CHRISTMAS

with Southern Living

INSPIRED IDEAS FOR HOLIDAY
COOKING & DECORATING

CHRISTMAS CHEERS! MENU, PAGE 72

2024
CHRISTMAS
with Southern Living

INSPIRED IDEAS FOR HOLIDAY
COOKING & DECORATING

Southern Living BOOKS

CONTENTS

DECK IT ALL!,
PAGE 24

MENU

A Classic Christmas

CHRISTMAS
CHEERS! MENU,
PAGE 72

Oh what fun!

Oh what fun it is to decorate the tree, host a Christmas party, and gather with family and friends this time of year! Whether you start with a theme, a color, or a beloved collection, decking your holiday halls provides a meaningful opportunity to showcase your style and set the stage for many memorable gatherings. Our stylists show you how to do just that with creative ideas for every room.

This book is a group effort that has been produced annually for half a century. It wouldn't happen without the many homeowners who graciously open their doors and allow us to set a festive stage for photography; talented prop stylists who spend weeks planning and prepping to make every space beautiful; food stylists who chop, whisk, and garnish so that recipes look as fabulous as they taste; and photographers who capture the holiday magic frame after frame. Cheers to them all!

I hope your holiday is filled with lots of magic, too.

Katherine Cobbs
EXECUTIVE EDITOR

1

DECORATE

HOLIDAY LOOKBOOK

GO DUTCH!

Holland's classic blue-and-white Delft
porcelain is a favorite of collectors in the
South and beyond. These high-contrast,
whimsical pieces provide the backdrop for
a fresh take on the traditional Christmas
palette. Mixing blue and white dishes,
vases, ornaments, and miniature canal
houses with forced bulbs and other blooms
provides an unexpected counterpoint for
customary holiday greenery.

It is Christmas in the heart that puts Christmas in the air.

— WILLIAM T. ELLIS

PATTERN PLAY

In the foyer, grass-cloth walls, intricate ironwork, and a puddling floral tablecloth provide an elegant backdrop for a wave of garland dressed up with velvet and satin ribbon and a pair of porcelain Dutch clogs hanging from the newel post. A mix of blue-and-white china vessels hold a blend of orchids, paperwhites, and Dutch bulbs in shades of purple, white, and cream. A waterfall of ornaments adds shimmer to the table.

BLUE CHRISTMAS

There is nothing melancholy about a glowing flocked tree dressed simply in a collection of blue-and-white ornaments, including hand-marbleized ones that are so simple to make (see how-to, page 179).

S

Simplicity is the name of the
crisp, clean decorating scheme
in the living room. It all starts
with the room's fireside focal
point. The mantel is dressed in
a swath of evergreen garland
accented with more of the
blue-and-white ornaments—
paint-marbleized glass orbs
mixed with ceramic bisque
stars—that grace the room's
flocked tree. Bespoke stockings
(see vendors, page 168)
trimmed in velvet ribbon hang
like icicles off of the marble
hearth's snowy mantelpiece.
Monogram-stamped ceramic
bisque charms personalize each
so there will be no confusion on
Christmas morning. Repeating
the hues of the room's existing
blue-and-white elements—
ginger jars, artwork, upholstery,
and fixtures—allows seasonal
additions and greenery
to be woven in seamlessly
for a merry mix.

WONDER WORKSHOP

Decking the halls takes planning and prep (see Holiday Planner, page 177), so dedicate a corner of the kitchen or mudroom to corral garden cuttings, flower bunches, potted plants, and supplies to make creating arrangements and cleaning up easy.

TINSEL AND TINFULS

Empty Dutch stroopwafel cookie tins are perfect for filling with candy or baked goods for giving, or use them as planters for mini trees to fit the blue-and-white theme.

SEASONAL SWAG

Garland and greenery are the stars of holiday decorating. Used to frame a window, evergreen boughs makes even a utilitarian workspace festive too.

It's not how much we give, but how much love we put into giving.

— MOTHER THERESA

FLOWER POWER

Like fireworks, a burst of amaryllis, roses, and ranunculus blossoms rises above a skirt of berries and branches in a sideboard arrangement that draws diners into the room for the Christmas feast.

MAKING SPIRITS BRIGHT

Once filled with Dutch genever, a juniper-based spirit, and offered to business travelers on KLM Airlines in the 1950s, Delft porcelain canal houses have become highly sought collectibles. Here, a grouping forms an idyllic blue-and-white Christmas village.

A PLACE FOR ALL

Rife with symbolism, hellebore stems rise from
moss-covered dishes and small seckel pears
grace each place at the table.
The many shades of green provide warm
contrast to cool blue-and-white china.

TULIP TREE

An heirloom Heinen Delfts Blau tulipiere filled with
nodding white parrot tulips, chartreuse-tinged
hellebores, and evergreen clippings brightens the
table when it's not set for a meal.

DECK IT ALL!

Whether you start with a theme, a color palette, or a beloved collection to highlight, decorating for the holidays provides an opportunity to embellish the pieces you have and let creativity blossom. Think beyond the tree, mantel, and door, and weave elements into unexpected spots for a dose of surprise around every corner.

OUTDOORS IN

Pieces from the garden brought indoors for winter keep branches and boughs fresh for use in decorating and add fitting natural whimsy to a conservatory table dressed for the season.

GARDEN GLOW

Glass hurricane lanterns hold an assortment of vintage oil lamps. Each looks like a colorful ornament, with lamp oil dyed sapphire blue, scarlet red, or verdant green, created by adding a few drops of food coloring to the oil in each lamp base.

This vignette takes a color cue from the striking backdrop of a series of framed John Derian prints.

A green sideboard pops against sherbet-color dining room walls. When not topped with a smorgasbord of holiday dishes, the garland- and wreath-accented piece is a festive focal point off of the main entry, holding gifts wrapped in a medley of block-print papers (see how-to, page 181) ready for delivery. More small packages stacked in a pyramid fashion with greenery tucked in the spaces between form an Advent tree, offering a surprise to unveil each day until Christmas.

*Christmas
waves
a magic
wand over
this world,
and behold,
everything
is softer
and more
beautiful.*

— NORMAN VINCENT PEALE

MOST WONDERFUL TIME

A Swedish Mora clock gets dressed up with
velvet ribbon, sugared fruit, and seeded
eucalyptus to complement the dining room
décor just beyond.

SHIMMER AND DINE

A china cabinet draped in an evergreen
shawl houses Christmas serving pieces for
entertaining throughout the season. A forest
of glass Christmas trees swirling with
glitter adds an elegant glow.

HOLIDAY NESTING

A decorative French birdcage gets gussied up for Christmas with gold-painted vines, a bevy of bows, and a miniature wreath for the door. An array of colorful bird ornaments suspended from the roof, roosting on bars, and resting in nests stand in for partridges, French hens, and turtle doves. In many cultures, birds and nests symbolize good luck and a happy home.

NOSTALGIC NOEL

A nostalgic noel awaits family and friends
at this joyful jewel of a historic home
brimming with prized collections, lush holiday
greenery, and doses of whimsy at every turn.
Waves of garland, a cascade of tinsel, and
a tree laden with gleaming ornaments take
guests back in time to Christmases past
while enjoying the contemporary comforts
of this well-appointed home.

Blessed is the season which engages the whole world in a conspiracy of love.

— HAMILTON WRIGHT MABIE

WHIMSICAL WELCOME

Swaths of fresh and faux greenery mingle to dress up this charming house that bursts with holiday cheer wherever you look. Red satin bows, dried citrus, and frosted pinecones add bursts of color to the mix decking the entry, draping the banister, and dressing the mantel. An antique Italian tole citrus tree rises to the ceiling beyond the banister. It is draped in dried citrus garland made by drying citrus slices on a rack set over a sheet pan in the oven at the lowest temperature for 3 to 4 hours. Insert a hook or tie with ribbon to use in your décor.

> *My favorite ornaments are vintage eggs with angels inside that my mother bought for a nickel each as a little girl.*
>
> – CARTER FELLERS, HOMEOWNER

COZY KITCHEN

The heartbeat of the home, the kitchen is a favorite gathering place. A counter seating area remains set with Christmas linens and dishes for lazy breakfasts and casual meals. Across the room, a bar with a silver gallery tray keeps cocktail-making tidy and out of the way. The red ticking-stripe curtain hides supplies.

LOVELY BRANCHES

Next to the fireplace, a tinsel-draped Christmas tree brims with heirloom and handmade ornaments, and new ones the homeowner adds to her collection each year.

LAYERED AND LOVELY

The vining floral Antoinette Poisson fabric wrapping the dining room walls provides a striking backdrop for family feasts. Candles, lamplight, and crystal add sparkle and glow to the table and sideboard, while the gilded chairs, mirror, and chandelier drive home the elegant formality of this Secret Garden setting. Evergreen garland accented with roses serves as a verdant runner on the table, mimicking the blossoms and vines on the walls.

SET FOR CELEBRATION

At one end of the dining room, a sunny seating area in front of a trio of windows provides a place to mingle before and linger after a meal. On the opposite side, a stately mantelpiece showcases a forest of bottlebrush trees that the homeowner has collected over the years. On the table, a layered mix of textures, colors, and botanicals gives each place setting a lush formality to match the surroundings.

FESTIVE FLOWER SHOW

Evergreen boughs are the belles of the holiday ball this time of year. But trees, topiaries, garlands, and wreaths can be made from flowers too. Think beyond the typical table centerpiece with these festive ways to incorporate buds, blossoms, branches, and berries into your holiday décor this season. Get the details for making each arrangement on the following pages, and see them displayed in party settings in the Entertain section on page 56.

TOOL SCHOOL

Floral designers'
secret weapons for
flower-arranging
finesse!

- □ Tote for tools and materials
- □ Mister or spray bottle
- □ Lighter or matches
- □ Florists wire
- □ Flower food
- □ Waxed wired twine
- □ Pruners
- □ Florists snips
- □ Flower frogs
- □ Florists shears
- □ Florists tape
- □ Wired wood picks
- □ Chicken wire
- □ Gardening gloves
- □ Apron with pockets*
- □ Pebbles*
- □ Water vials*
- □ Natural floral foam*

*not shown

**GRATEFUL
GATHERING MENU,
PAGE 58**

GRATEFUL GATHERING FLOWERS

This fabulous fall arrangement celebrates seasonal color with fiery-leaved branches and bare deciduous ones rising from a bounty of blooms in shades of pink, purple, orange, and scarlet. Pumpkins of all sizes, gilded and left natural, including the creamy white variety used as the vase, complete the scene.

materials list

Cake stand

Bowls

White 'Cotton Candy' pumpkin

Small 'Baby Boo' and 'Jack-Be-Little' pumpkins

Gold-leaf papers or metallic paint

Paintbrushes

Bradford pear 'Autumn Blaze' branches (*Pyrus calleryana*)

Burgundy peony 'Armani' and pink peony
'Sarah Bernhardt' (*Paeonia lactiflora*)

Red pussy willow 'Mt. Asama' branches
(*Salix chaenomeloides*)

Purple common stock (*Matthiola incana*)

Pink waxflower (*Chamelaucium uncinatum*)

Magenta calla lily 'Garnet Glow' and orange 'Flame'
(*Zantedeschia aethiopica*)

Blush spray roses (*Rosa spp. and hybrid*)

NOTE: *The spray rose gets its name for the multiple blooms produced on a single stem. Though the blossoms are somewhat smaller than other rose varieties, the showy display is no less impressive.*

CHRISTMAS CHEERS! FLOWERS

Just a few plant materials are all it takes to make this striking holiday display. A trio of the same minimalist arrangement delivers a lush, abundant look for the cocktail party table. Each is easily relocated to brighten spots around the house after the guests depart. A solid base is the key to success here. Use florists tape to secure dampened floral foam or crumpled chicken wire in the bowls and cover with moss. Wire tender stems with florists picks to strengthen them so they do not break when arranged. Alternatively, use pebbles to secure stems.

materials list

Bowls

Natural floral foam, chicken wire, or pebbles

Florists tape

Florists picks to fortify stems

Sphagnum moss sheets (*Sphagnum capillifolium*)

Mexican cypress (*Cupressus*)

Paperwhite stems (*Narcissus papyraceus*)

Winterberry branches (*Ilex verticillata*)

Brass garland

Riser

CHRISTMAS
CHEERS! MENU,
PAGE 72

FEEL-GOOD
FEAST MENU,
PAGE 82

FEEL-GOOD FEAST FLOWERS

Lush and full, the hero of this abundant display—creamy white amaryllis—bursts forth and cascades over the edge of the container. The velvety copper backsides of glossy green magnolia leaves repeat the warm patina of the vase. Dainty Queen Anne's lace and Rocket Larkspur stems rise above a showy understory of purple sea holly, hemlock, scabiosa, and privet berry for a holiday showstopper that is anything but traditional.

materials list

Copper vessel

Blue ceramic vases

Copper ball ornaments

Amaryllis 'White Nymph' (*Hippeastrum*)

Southern magnolia (*Magnolia grandiflora*)

White scabiosa daisy (*Scabiosa caucasica*)

Rocket larkspur (*Consolida*)

Queen Anne's lace (*Daucus carota*)

Alpine sea holly (*Eryngium*)

Eastern hemlock (*Tsuga*)

Privet berry (*Ligustrum vulgare*)

NOTE: *Powdered flower food, or floral preservative, helps hydrate cut flowers and cut down on bacterial growth in the water, which makes arrangements last longer. However, it is critical to measure and mix properly. The ideal ratio is 2 teaspoons of flower food to 4 cups of water. Make the mixture in advance and chill it to fill vases with open blooms you want to last. Mix the flower food with slightly warm water to urge the blooms to fully open. Once flowers bloom, change the water to the chilled mix for longevity.*

CLASSIC CHRISTMAS SUPPER FLOWERS

Pink milk glass mixing bowls nestle on risers from largest to smallest to create a treelike structure with ample room for a fun combination of plant textures and types. An iridescent glass tree used as a topper drives home the blooming tree approach. The retro pastel palette is reminiscent of sugared fruit, pink noses, mercury glass, and Shiny Brite ornaments and delivers heaps of nostalgia to any setting.

materials list

Pink milk glass mixing bowls

Risers

Pink poinsettias 'J'Adore Soft Pink'
(*Poinsettia euphorbia pulcherrima*)

Blush spray roses (*Rosa spp. and hybrid*)

Dusty miller (*Jacobaea maritima*)

Pink pepperberry (*Schinus terebinthifolia*)

Pink hypericum berry (*Hypericum androsaemum*)

Pink waxflower (*Chamelaucium uncinatum*)

Fraser fir branches (*Abies fraseri*)

Shortleaf pine branches (*Pinus echinata*)

Tray

Crystal candlesticks with taper candles

Wrapped packages

CLASSIC
CHRISTMAS
SUPPER MENU,
PAGE 90

ENTERTAIN

HOLIDAY MENUS

**GRATEFUL GATHERING
FLOWERS HOW-TO,
PAGE 49**

GRATEFUL GATHERING

menu

Tipsy Turkey Cocktail
Jammy Gorgonzola Bites
Caramelized Apple-Onion Soup
Autumn Beet Salad
Sorghum-Brined Roast Chicken
Mixed Mushroom Sauté
Candied Butternut Squash with Fried Sage
Pear Bread Pudding with Brandy Sauce

Autumn's cool days and crisp nights usher in gratitude
for the festive season that is just around the bend. As
Mother Nature changes her wardrobe, harvests change
too. Cool-season ingredients shine in roasts
and long-simmered stews—perfect dishes for a fall
feast with friends or the Thanksgiving table.

TIPSY TURKEY COCKTAIL

ACTIVE **10 MIN.**

TOTAL **10 MIN.** • SERVES **1**

Amaro Nonino is an herbaceous grappa-based Italian bitter with flavors of caramel, apricot, bitter orange, thyme, saffron, and wormwood. It adds a complexity to this cocktail that is hard to replicate with a substitute. Make a batch of simple syrup to keep on hand during the holidays for sweetening beverages.

3 Tbsp. (1½ oz.) Wild Turkey bourbon

3 Tbsp. (1½ oz.) pomegranate juice

1 Tbsp. plus 1 tsp. (¾ oz.) Amaro Nonino

1 Tbsp. (½ oz.) Simple Syrup (recipe follows)

1 Tbsp. (½ oz.) lime juice

Lime wheel

Pomegranate seeds

Combine first 5 ingredients in a cocktail shaker with ice and shake vigorously. Strain into a glass over fresh ice. Garnish with a lime wheel and pomegranate seeds.

SIMPLE SYRUP

Combine 1 cup sugar and 1 cup water in a small saucepan. Cook over medium, stirring constantly, until sugar dissolves. Makes 1 cup

. . . .

Fresh Pomegranate How-To

You can buy pomegranate seeds, or arils, in containers in the produce section, but seeding a pomegranate isn't tricky. It doesn't have to stain your fingers or counters either. Arils keep in the fridge for two weeks and in the freezer for several months.

1. Cut off the top and end of the fruit, then use a knife to score the skin into four sections.

2. Place the pomegranate in a bowl of water; break the shell apart along the scored lines.

3. Use your fingers to loosen the arils under water; the seeds will sink, and the white membrane will float. Toss the membrane.

4. Strain through a sieve to catch arils. Use them wherever a juicy, sweet-tart dose of crunch is welcome or as directed in your recipe.

. . . .

JAMMY GORGONZOLA BITES

ACTIVE **10 MIN.**

TOTAL **15 MIN.** • MAKES **2 DOZEN**

These crunchy, savory-sweet bites pack a wallop of flavor. Frozen phyllo shells and a jar of jam make quick work of these addictive nibbles. Serve them hot from the oven to wow your crowd.

24 mini phyllo pastry shells, thawed

2 Tbsp. red currant jam, plus more for garnish

1 (6-oz.) pkg. cream Gorgonzola crumbles

¼ cup chopped pecans

1 tsp. flaky sea salt

Fresh rosemary leaves

1. Preheat oven to 350°F. Arrange pastry shells on a rimmed baking sheet.

2. Spoon ¼ tsp. jam into each shell; top evenly with about 1 Tbsp. Gorgonzola crumbles. Sprinkle with about ½ tsp. chopped pecans.

3. Bake at 350°F until cheese is melted, 7 to 8 minutes. Sprinkle with salt and top with a dollop of extra jam for color, if desired. Top each with a few fresh rosemary leaves. Serve immediately.

CARAMELIZED APPLE-ONION SOUP

ACTIVE **1 HOUR, 10 MIN.**

TOTAL **2 HOURS** • SERVES **6 TO 8**

Slowly caramelizing onions in butter over low heat coaxes out their sweetness and adds a deeper flavor to this ever-so-sweet fall soup. Garnish with store-bought seasoned croutons or crunchy cheese crisps for a textural counterpoint.

2 Tbsp. butter

2 medium-size sweet onions, thinly sliced

1 garlic clove

1 bay leaf

2 medium-size Pink Lady or Jazz apples, peeled and cut into ¼-inch-thick slices

6 cups chicken broth

½ cup apple cider

1 medium-size russet potato, peeled and cut into ¼-inch-thick slices

½ cup heavy cream

1 Tbsp. fresh lemon juice

1½ to 2 tsp. kosher salt

1 tsp. freshly ground black pepper

Croutons

Chopped fresh parsley

l. Melt butter in a large Dutch oven over low heat. Add onions and next 2 ingredients, and cook, stirring often, 30 to 35 minutes or until onions are caramel-color. (Adjust heat to prevent scorching.) Add apples, and cook, stirring often, 5 minutes. Add broth and next 2 ingredients. Increase heat to medium, and bring to a boil, stirring occasionally. Reduce heat to medium-low, and simmer, stirring occasionally, 20 to 25 minutes or until apples and potato are tender. Remove from heat, and let stand 15 minutes. Discard bay leaf.

2. Process mixture with a handheld blender until smooth. Add cream and lemon juice. Return to low heat; simmer, stirring often, 15 minutes. Add salt and pepper. Serve topped with croutons and parsley.

AUTUMN BEET SALAD

ACTIVE **35 MIN.**

TOTAL **5 HOURS** • SERVES **6 TO 8**

Perfectly balanced with different flavors, textures, and colors, this salad is a jewel-tone addition to any fall spread.

1 lb. orange and yellow beets, peeled and thinly sliced into half-moons

½ cup white balsamic vinegar

½ cup champagne vinegar

5 Tbsp. maple syrup

2 tsp. kosher salt

½ medium-size sweet onion, cut into thin strips

½ cup extra-virgin olive oil

2 Tbsp. white wine vinegar

1 tsp. grainy Dijon mustard

6 thick applewood-smoked bacon slices, cooked and crumbled

1 Jazz apple (about 8 oz.), thinly sliced

3 cups firmly packed baby arugula

3 cups loosely packed green leaf lettuce, torn

½ cup loosely packed fresh chervil or flat-leaf parsley leaves

¼ cup toasted chopped pecans

l. Microwave beets and water to cover in a microwave-safe bowl at HIGH 8 to 10 minutes or until crisp-tender. Let stand 30 minutes. Drain and rinse beets.

2. Stir together white balsamic vinegar, champagne vinegar, maple syrup, salt, and 2 Tbsp. water; pour into a large zip-top plastic freezer bag. Add beets and onion. Seal and chill 4 hours.

3. Drain beets and onion, reserving ⅓ cup pickling liquid. Discard remaining liquid. Whisk together olive oil, next 2 ingredients, and reserved ⅓ cup pickling liquid until smooth. Add salt and pepper to taste. Toss together bacon, remaining 5 ingredients, and desired amount of dressing. Serve with beets, onions, and remaining dressing.

SORGHUM-BRINED ROAST CHICKEN

ACTIVE **45 MIN.** • TOTAL **8 HOURS, 25 MIN.** • SERVES **8**

*This brined, roasted chicken is juicy, rich, and delicious, but the flavorful gravy is worth the effort.
Buy airline breasts (first wing joint attached) for a pretty presentation. Fuyu persimmons,
reminiscent of fall pumpkins, are a lovely garnish for the platter.*

½ cup kosher salt

½ cup sorghum syrup or light
 brown sugar

2 cups ice cubes

1 sweet onion, thinly sliced

2 fresh marjoram sprigs

2 garlic cloves, peeled and
 sliced

½ tsp. black peppercorns

8 chicken breasts, airline cut

½ tsp. garlic salt

2 Tbsp. canola oil, divided

8 garlic cloves, unpeeled,
 divided

2 fresh marjoram sprigs,
 divided, plus more for garnish

Make-Ahead Bourbon-Apple
 Gravy (recipe follows)

1. Bring 4 cups water to a boil in a Dutch oven over medium-high heat. Add kosher salt and sorghum syrup. Reduce heat to low, and simmer, stirring occasionally, 2 to 3 minutes or until salt and sorghum syrup dissolve. Transfer to a very large bowl; add ice and next 4 ingredients. Let stand, stirring occasionally, 30 minutes or until mixture cools to room temperature. Cover and chill 30 minutes to 1 hour or until cold.

2. Submerge chicken in cold brine. Cover and chill 6 to 8 hours.

3. Preheat oven to 400°F. Remove chicken from brine; rinse and pat dry. Sprinkle with garlic salt.

4. Heat 1 Tbsp. oil in a 14-inch cast-iron skillet over medium-high heat. Add 4 unpeeled garlic cloves, 1 marjoram sprig, and half of chicken. Cook 5 minutes or until skin is browned and crisp. (The sorghum in the brine will brown the skin quickly.) Turn chicken and garlic, and cook 5 minutes or until browned. Remove chicken, and place on a wire rack in a jelly-roll pan. Wipe skillet clean and repeat with remaining oil, chicken, garlic, and marjoram sprig.

5. Bake chicken, skin side up, at 400°F for 10 to 20 minutes or until a meat thermometer inserted into thickest portion registers 165°F. (Check internal temperature after 10 minutes to avoid overcooking). Cover with foil. Let stand 10 minutes before slicing. Serve with Make-Ahead Bourbon-Apple Gravy and additional marjoram, if desired.

MAKE-AHEAD BOURBON-APPLE GRAVY

¼ cup apple cider

2 to 3 Tbsp. bourbon or apple
 cider

Mix of jus from roasted
 chicken and chicken broth

¼ cup butter

⅓ cup all-purpose flour

1. Combine cider and bourbon; add enough jus and broth to equal 2 cups.

2. Melt butter in a saucepan and whisk in flour. Cook and stir over medium 1 minute. Stir in broth mixture. Cook and stir over medium until thickened and bubbly. Cook and stir 1 minute more. Season with kosher salt and black pepper. Serve warm or transfer to an airtight container and refrigerate up to 3 days. Reheat gravy in a saucepan. Makes about 1¾ cups

MIXED MUSHROOM SAUTÉ

ACTIVE **35 MIN.**

TOTAL **35 MIN.** • SERVES **8**

Any variety of mushroom works well here. Sear the sliced and chopped mushrooms in batches, without crowding, in a hot skillet so that they take on golden color without steaming.

1 (8-oz.) pkg. stemmed and sliced fresh shiitake mushrooms

4½ Tbsp. olive oil, divided

2 large portobello mushrooms (about 8 oz.), stemmed, cleaned, and chopped

1 (8-oz.) pkg. stemmed and sliced oyster mushrooms*

2 Tbsp. butter

3 Tbsp. minced shallots

2 garlic cloves, chopped

½ tsp. kosher salt

½ tsp. freshly ground black pepper

3 tsp. sliced fresh chives

1. Cook shiitake mushrooms in a single layer in 1½ Tbsp. hot oil in a 10- to 12-inch nonstick skillet over high heat, stirring often, 4 to 6 minutes or until browned. Transfer to a medium bowl. Repeat procedure two more times with portobello mushrooms, oyster mushrooms, and remaining oil.

2. Melt butter in skillet over medium-high heat; add shallots, and sauté 2 to 3 minutes or until tender. Stir in garlic; cook 1 minute. Add mushrooms, salt, and pepper; toss gently to coat. Remove from heat; stir in chives. Serve warm.

*Cremini or button mushrooms may be substituted.

CANDIED BUTTERNUT SQUASH WITH FRIED SAGE

ACTIVE **20 MIN.**

TOTAL **45 MIN.** • SERVES **8 TO 12**

This simple preparation calls for a clever technique. Create more surface area for caramelization to work magic by scoring the squash flesh with a sharp knife. Caramelization equals flavor!

1 butternut squash (3 to 4 lb.), halved, seeded, and cut into 2-inch wedges

½ cup melted butter

3 Tbsp. light brown sugar

Table salt

Freshly ground black pepper

Fried Sage (recipe follows)

1. Preheat oven to 450°F. Score a crisscross pattern ¼ inch deep into squash flesh, using a sharp knife.

2. Stir together butter and light brown sugar until sugar dissolves. Brush one-third of butter mixture over all sides of squash. Place squash, flesh sides down, in a lightly greased aluminum foil-lined 15- x 10-inch jelly-roll pan.

3. Bake at 450°F for 10 minutes. Turn squash over; spread with half of remaining butter mixture. Bake 12 to 14 minutes or until tender. Remove from oven; increase oven temperature to broil. Brush squash with remaining butter mixture. Broil 2 to 3 minutes or until well caramelized. Sprinkle with salt and pepper to taste and top with Fried Sage. Serve warm.

FRIED SAGE

Heat ¼ cup canola oil in a small skillet over medium-high. Fry 24 sage leaves in batches, 6 to 8 leaves at a time, for 5 to 7 seconds. Do not let brown. Transfer with a fork to paper towels. Sprinkle generously with flaky salt. Use at once, or store between layers of paper towels in an airtight container at room temperature for up to 1 day. Makes 2 dozen

PEAR BREAD PUDDING WITH BRANDY SAUCE

ACTIVE 25 MIN. • TOTAL 2 HOURS, 30 MIN., INCLUDING SAUCE AND PEARS • SERVES 8 TO 10

Serve this family-style from a baking dish, or divide with a 3-inch round cutter for a uniform, elegant presentation.

2 Tbsp. unsalted butter

3 large Bartlett pears (about 1½ lb.), peeled and cut into ¼- to ½-inch cubes

3 cups heavy cream

4 large eggs

1 large egg yolk

¼ cup granulated sugar

1 tsp. pumpkin pie spice

1 (16-oz.) cinnamon-raisin bread loaf, cut into ¾-inch cubes

4 Tbsp. light brown sugar, divided

Brandy Sauce (recipe follows)

Sautéed Pears (recipe follows)

l. Preheat oven to 375°F. Melt butter in a large nonstick skillet over medium-high heat; add pears, and cook, stirring occasionally, 8 to 10 minutes or until softened and lightly browned.

2. Whisk together cream and next 4 ingredients in a large bowl until smooth. Stir in bread cubes; let stand 5 minutes. Stir in cooked pears.

3. Sprinkle 2 Tbsp. light brown sugar into a buttered 13- x 9-inch baking dish. Add bread-and-pear mixture to dish, and spread in an even layer. Sprinkle with remaining 2 Tbsp. light brown sugar.

4. Bake at 375°F for 40 to 45 minutes or until light golden and center is set. (Bread pudding will puff to top of dish and pull away slightly from sides as it bakes.) Cool 10 minutes. Serve warm with Brandy Sauce and Sautéed Pears.

BRANDY SAUCE

Whisk together 1 cup heavy cream, 2 large egg yolks, and ¼ cup sugar in a 2-qt. saucepan, and cook over medium heat, whisking constantly (so mixture doesn't scorch or scramble), 8 to 10 minutes or until mixture thinly coats back of a wooden spoon. Pour through a fine wire-mesh strainer into a bowl. Stir in 2 Tbsp. brandy or cognac. Add 1 cinnamon stick, if desired. Fill a large bowl with ice. Place bowl containing cream mixture in ice, and let stand, stirring occasionally, 30 minutes to cool. Remove cinnamon stick. Cover and chill 1 hour to 3 days. Makes about 1⅓ cups

SAUTÉED PEARS

Melt 2 Tbsp. butter in a large skillet over medium heat; add 2 large Bartlett pears, diced; sauté 2 minutes. Stir in 3 Tbsp. sugar and 2 tsp. fresh lemon juice. Cook, stirring often, 6 to 8 minutes or until golden. Makes about 2 cups

CHRISTMAS CHEERS
FLOWERS HOW-TO,
PAGE 50

CHRISTMAS CHEERS!

menu

Big Batch Boulevardier Cocktails
Rosemary-Brown Butter Pecans
Asparagus and Shrimp with Lemon-Dill Vinaigrette
Crispy Artichoke Hearts with Harissa Aioli
Ham and Tomato Chutney Biscuits with Gruyère Butter
Almond Snowballs
Bourbon-Caramel Truffles

Kick off the season and show off your decked halls and
holiday table by hosting a festive open house.
A seasonal cocktail and bevy of delicious appetizers
will put smiles on the faces of everyone gathered and
allow you to mix and mingle or play Kris Kringle.

BIG BATCH BOULEVARDIER COCKTAILS

ACTIVE **5 MIN.**

TOTAL **5 MIN., PLUS CHILLING**

MAKES **12 (4-OZ.) DRINKS**

Like a negroni, only swapping bourbon for the usual gin, you can make and bottle this big-batch cocktail a week (or even two) before your party.

2¼ cups (18 oz.) bourbon

1½ cups (12 oz.) sweet vermouth

1½ cups (12 oz.) Campari

½ cup (4 oz.) water

Fresh rosemary sprigs

Clementine slices

Combine everything in a large pot or bowl and transfer to 2 (750-ml) bottles. Seal and chill until ready to serve. Serve 4-oz. pours over ice in short glasses. Garnish with rosemary sprigs and clementine slices.

ROSEMARY-BROWN BUTTER PECANS

ACTIVE **15 MIN.**

TOTAL **1 HOUR** • MAKES **4 CUPS**

Double this for a crowd or for gifting.

¼ cup salted butter

4 cups shelled pecan halves

1 tsp. table salt

2 tsp. dark brown sugar

1 Tbsp. chopped fresh rosemary

1. Preheat oven to 350°F. Cook butter in a saucepan over medium heat, stirring constantly, 3 to 5 minutes or just until butter begins to turn golden brown. Remove pan from heat; stir in pecans and arrange in a single layer on a baking sheet. Sprinkle with salt and brown sugar.

2. Bake at 350°F for 10 to 12 minutes or until toasted and fragrant, stirring halfway through. Sprinkle with rosemary. Bake 2 minutes. Cool completely on baking sheet (about 30 minutes). Store in an airtight container.

ASPARAGUS AND SHRIMP WITH LEMON-DILL VINAIGRETTE

ACTIVE **10 MIN.**

TOTAL **15 MIN.** • SERVES **8 TO 10**

Save time by purchasing cooked, peeled shrimp at the seafood counter; or quickly thaw frozen cooked, peeled shrimp in a colander under cold running water.

2 lb. fresh asparagus, cut into 2-inch pieces and blanched

2 lb. cooked, peeled medium shrimp

Lemon-Dill Vinaigrette (recipe follows)

2 oz. pecorino cheese, shaved

Arrange asparagus and shrimp on a platter. Drizzle with a bit of the vinaigrette and top with shaved pecorino. Serve remaining vinaigrette on the side.

LEMON-DILL VINAIGRETTE

Whisk together 1 cup olive oil, 3 Tbsp. chopped fresh dill, 4 tsp. lemon zest, ½ cup fresh lemon juice, 2 tsp. Dijon mustard, and ½ tsp. sugar. Season with salt and pepper to taste. Serve immediately, or store in an airtight container in refrigerator up to 3 days. Makes 1½ cups

A Classic Christmas

CRISPY ARTICHOKE HEARTS
WITH HARISSA AIOLI

ACTIVE **35 MIN.** • TOTAL **35 MIN.** • MAKES **ABOUT 2 DOZEN**

Harissa, a savory chile-garlic paste flavored with spices, vinegar, and olive oil, adds lots of flavor to the dipping sauce for these crunchy artichoke hearts.

HARISSA AIOLI

1 cup mayonnaise

¼ cup full-fat plain Greek yogurt

2 tsp. fresh lemon juice (from 1 lemon)

¾ tsp. kosher salt

1 (6.7-oz.) jar harissa

2 Tbsp. finely chopped fresh parsley

CRISPY ARTICHOKE HEARTS

Canola oil

½ cup all-purpose flour

2 large eggs, lightly beaten

2 Tbsp. whole buttermilk

1½ cups panko breadcrumbs

1 tsp. kosher salt, plus more to taste

½ tsp. black pepper, plus more to taste

1 (24-oz.) jar marinated quartered artichoke hearts, drained and thoroughly patted dry

Chopped fresh parsley

1. Prepare the Harissa Aioli: Stir together mayonnaise, yogurt, lemon juice, salt, and harissa in a medium bowl. Stir in parsley. Cover; chill until ready to serve. (Harissa Aioli can be stored in an airtight container in the refrigerator for up to 1 week.)

2. Prepare the Crispy Artichoke Hearts: Pour oil to a depth of 2 inches in a large Dutch oven; heat oil over medium to 350°F. Place flour in a medium bowl. Stir together eggs and buttermilk in a separate medium bowl until well combined. Stir together panko, 1 tsp. salt, and ½ tsp. pepper in a third medium bowl. Working in batches, toss artichoke heart quarters in flour until well coated. Transfer to egg mixture, and toss to coat. Place in panko mixture, and toss again to coat; place on a baking sheet lined with parchment paper.

3. Working in 3 batches, fry artichoke hearts in hot oil, stirring occasionally, until golden brown, about 1 minute and 30 seconds; drain on a baking sheet lined with paper towels, and immediately season to taste with salt and pepper. Keep warm in a 200°F oven. Allow oil to return to 350°F between batches. Garnish with chopped fresh parsley. Serve hot with Harissa Aioli for dipping.

HAM AND TOMATO CHUTNEY BISCUITS WITH GRUYÈRE BUTTER

ACTIVE **15 MIN.** • TOTAL **4 HOURS, 50 MIN.** • MAKES **20 APPETIZER SERVINGS**

Grab a bottle of your favorite spicy ginger ale (such as Blenheim from South Carolina or Buffalo Rock from Alabama) for this recipe. Frozen buttermilk biscuits and store-bought chutney simplify the party prep.

1 (8- to 9-lb.) smoked, ready-to-cook bone-in ham

2 (12-oz.) bottles or cans spicy ginger ale

½ cup bourbon

¼ cup firmly packed dark brown sugar

2 tsp. coarsely ground black pepper

½ tsp. kosher salt

½ tsp. dry mustard

¼ tsp. ground red pepper

20 frozen buttermilk biscuits

1 cup tomato chutney, such as Alecia's Tomato Chutney

Gruyère Butter (recipe follows)

1. Preheat oven to 325°F. Remove skin from ham. Trim fat to ¼-inch thickness. Make shallow cuts in fat 1 inch apart in a diamond pattern. Place ham, fat side up, in a roasting pan; add ginger ale and bourbon to pan. Cover loosely with foil.

2. Bake, covered, at 325°F for 4 to 4½ hours or until a meat thermometer inserted into ham registers 140°F, basting with pan juices every 30 minutes.

3. Stir together brown sugar and next 4 ingredients. Remove ham from oven; uncover and sprinkle sugar mixture over ham, lightly pressing mixture into fat.

4. Bake, uncovered, at 325°F for 20 to 25 minutes or until crust is browned and a meat thermometer registers 145°F. Transfer ham to a cutting board, and let stand 15 minutes before carving.

5. While ham rests, prepare biscuits. Raise oven temperature to 350°F and arrange frozen biscuits side-by-side on a nonstick baking sheet; bake 20 to 25 minutes, or per package instructions. Slice biscuits horizontally.

6. Carve ham and arrange alongside sliced biscuits on a platter. Serve with tomato chutney and Gruyère Butter for spreading.

GRUYÈRE BUTTER

3 oz. Gruyère, finely grated

½ cup butter, softened

1 green onion, minced

1 tsp. minced fresh rosemary

1 tsp. grainy Dijon mustard

¼ tsp. freshly ground black pepper

Stir together all ingredients with a fork until thoroughly blended. Serve immediately. Store in refrigerator up to 1 week. Makes 1 cup

ALMOND SNOWBALLS

ACTIVE **50 MIN.**

TOTAL **1 HOUR, 35 MIN.** • MAKES **5 DOZEN**

This makes more than required for this menu, so package some up for guests to take home as a holiday party favor treat.

½ cup slivered almonds

1 cup butter, softened

1 tsp. almond extract

1½ cups powdered sugar, divided

2½ cups all-purpose flour

¼ tsp. salt

Parchment paper

1. Preheat oven to 350 F. Bake almonds in a single layer in a shallow pan 6 minutes or until toasted and fragrant, stirring halfway through. Cool completely (about 20 minutes). Reduce oven temperature to 325 F.

2. Process almonds in a food processor 30 seconds or until finely ground.

3. Beat butter at medium speed with a heavy duty electric stand mixer until creamy. Add almond extract, then gradually and 1 cup powdered sugar, beating well. (Dough will be crumbly.)

4. Combine flour, salt, and almonds; gradually add to butter mixture, beating until blended. Shape dough into ¾-inch balls, and place 2 inches apart on parchment paper lined baking sheets.

5. Bake at 325 F for 12 to 15 minutes or until edges are lightly browned. Cool on baking sheets 2 minutes. Transfer to wire racks, and cool 10 minutes. Roll cookies in remaining ½ cup powdered sugar.

BOURBON-CARAMEL TRUFFLES

ACTIVE **30 MIN.**

TOTAL **2 HOURS, 30 MIN.** • MAKES **3 DOZEN**

The melt-in-your-mouth velvety quality of these rich truffles comes from the cane syrup and evaporated milk instead of heavy creamy, which also allows the other flavors shine through.

6 Tbsp. brown sugar

4 Tbsp. evaporated whole milk

2 Tbsp. golden cane syrup

⅛ tsp. table salt

2 Tbsp. bourbon

1 tsp. vanilla extract

7 oz. bittersweet chocolate, finely chopped

3.5 oz. milk chocolate, finely chopped

¼ cup unsweetened cocoa powder

1. Combine first 4 ingredients in a saucepan over medium-high heat; bring to a boil. Cook 1 minute or until sugar dissolves. Remove from heat. Stir in bourbon and vanilla. Add chopped chocolates; let stand 1 minute. Stir until smooth. Pour into a shallow dish; cover and chill 2 hours.

2. Heat a 1 tablespoon measuring spoon with hot water; pat dry. Scoop chocolate mixture with spoon; dip in cocoa powder. Roll into balls. Refrigerate until ready to serve.

FEEL-GOOD FEAST
FLOWERS HOW-TO,
PAGE 53

FEEL-GOOD FEAST

menu

Vermouth Cocktail
Crudités Wreath with Creamy Hazelnut Dip
Slow-Cooker Beef Stew
Flaky Dinner Rolls
Chocolatey Christmas Pudding Pie

Aromas of a simmering stew wafting from the kitchen prime palates and beckon family and friends to the table. It's the time to reconnect and linger over a comforting meal that you can prep ahead and forget about—only it's so delicious no one else will.

VERMOUTH COCKTAIL

ACTIVE **1 MIN.**

TOTAL **1 MIN.** • SERVES **1**

Low in alcohol and at just 64 calories per serving, this is a steady sipper guests can enjoy all afternoon. It also stimulates appetites for the meal to come.

¼ cup (2 oz.) Dolin red vermouth

¼ cup (2 oz.) chilled club soda

Orange slice

Combine red vermouth with club soda over ice and garnish with orange slice.

CRUDITÉS WREATH WITH CREAMY HAZELNUT DIP

ACTIVE **15 MIN.**

TOTAL **15 MIN.** • SERVES **12 TO 16**

Blanch the broccoli florets and green beans in boiling salted water for about 1 minute to keep this verdant veggie round-up bright green. Transfer to an ice bath to cool quickly. Drain and pat dry on a towel. Do the same for the Romanesco florets, but blanch for 3 minutes.

1½ cups raw, unsalted shelled hazelnuts (7 oz.)

1 large shallot, minced

¼ cup white wine vinegar

1 cup mayonnaise

1 Tbsp. fresh lemon juice

1 Tbsp. fresh orange juice

1 large garlic clove, minced

½ cup lemon-infused olive oil, plus more for garnish

2 cups sour cream

2 Tbsp. minced parsley

2 Tbsp. minced fresh tarragon

2 Tbsp. finely sliced fresh chives

Salt and freshly ground black pepper

6 cups broccoli florets or broccolini stalks, blanched

3 cups green beans, (12 oz.) blanched

2 heads Romanesco, cut into florets (about 6 cups), blanched

12 fresh shishito or banana peppers

12 cherry or grape tomatoes

1. Preheat oven to 350°F. Spread hazelnuts on a large rimmed baking sheet. Toast 8 minutes. Let cool. Transfer to a food processor and pulse until coarsely ground.

2. Combine shallot and vinegar in a small bowl. Set aside 10 minutes. Whisk mayonnaise, lemon juice, orange juice, and garlic in a large bowl. Gradually whisk in oil until thickened.

3. Drain shallot and stir into mayonnaise. Stir in sour cream and herbs. Stir in the ground hazelnuts and season with salt and pepper. Scrape dip into a serving bowl. Garnish with additional oil and black pepper, if desired.

4. Arrange crudités in wreath fashion. Cluster tomatoes in several places as a nod to holly berries. Serve the bowl of dip in the center.

SLOW-COOKER BEEF STEW

ACTIVE **35 MIN.**

TOTAL **8 HOURS, 35 MIN.** • SERVES **6 TO 8**

This stew swaps the usual red wine for a dry white for a more nuanced flavor. This cooks to perfection as you go about your holiday errands. It's actually best made a day or two before serving to give the herbs and wine time to meld with the meat and vegetables for rich, complex flavor. Just gently reheat to serve. To end up with 2 pounds trimmed chuck roast, you should purchase 2½ pounds. Serve this Beef Bourguignonne-style over cooked egg noodles.

1 Tbsp. canola oil

2 lb. trimmed boneless chuck roast, cut into 1-inch pieces

1 cup dry white wine

¼ cup unsalted tomato paste

1¼ tsp. kosher salt

1 tsp. freshly ground black pepper

6 large carrots, cut diagonally into 1½- to 2-inch pieces (about 1 lb.)

1 cup thick-sliced mushrooms

6 large garlic cloves, minced (about 2 Tbsp.)

5 celery stalks, cut diagonally into 1-inch pieces

1 (12-oz.) pkg. frozen pearl onions

2½ cups unsalted beef stock, divided

6 large thyme sprigs

3 bay leaves

3½ Tbsp. all-purpose flour

3 oz. pitted niçoise olives

Fresh flat-leaf parsley leaves (optional)

Cooked egg noodles

1. Heat oil in large skillet over medium-high. Add half of beef to skillet; cook, turning to brown on all sides, about 8 minutes. Place in a 5- to 6-qt. slow cooker. Repeat procedure with remaining beef. Add wine to skillet; scrape to loosen browned bits from bottom of pan. Bring wine to a boil, and cook 1 minute. Add to slow cooker. Stir in tomato paste, salt, pepper, carrots, mushrooms, garlic, celery, frozen onions, and 2 cups beef stock. Add thyme sprigs and bay leaves. Cover and cook on LOW until beef is tender, 7½ to 8 hours.

2. Whisk together flour and remaining ½ cup stock. Add flour mixture and olives to slow cooker. Increase heat to HIGH; cover and cook until bubbly and thickened, about 5 minutes. Discard thyme sprigs and bay leaves. Garnish with parsley, if desired. Serve over egg noodles.

FLAKY DINNER ROLLS

ACTIVE **40 MIN.**

TOTAL **2 HOURS, 15 MIN.** • MAKES **1 DOZEN**

Milk and sugar add richness to this "rough puff" laminated dough.

3 Tbsp. sugar

1 pkg. dry yeast (about 2¼ tsp.)

1 cup warm fat-free milk (100°F to 110°F)

13.5 oz. all-purpose flour (about 3 cups), divided

¾ tsp. salt

5 Tbsp. butter, softened, divided

Cooking spray

1. Dissolve sugar and yeast in warm milk in a large bowl; let stand 5 minutes. Spoon flour into dry measuring cups; level with a knife. Add 2¾ cups flour and the salt to yeast mixture; stir until a dough forms. Turn dough out onto a lightly floured surface. Knead until smooth (about 5 minutes); add flour, 1 Tbsp. at a time, to prevent dough from sticking to hands (dough will feel slightly sticky). Cover with plastic wrap; let rest for 10 minutes.

2. Roll the dough into a 12- x 10-inch rectangle on a lightly floured baking sheet. Gently spread 3 Tbsp. butter over dough. Working with a long side, fold up bottom third of dough. Fold top third over the first fold to form a 12- x 3-inch rectangle. Cover with plastic wrap; place in freezer for 10 minutes.

3. Remove dough and plastic wrap. Roll on baking sheet (sprinkle on a little more flour, if needed), into a 12- x 10-inch rectangle. Working with a long side, fold up bottom third of dough. Fold top third over the first fold to form a 12- x 3-inch rectangle. Cover with plastic wrap; place in freezer for 10 minutes.

4. Melt remaining 2 Tbsp. butter. Remove dough and plastic wrap. Roll on baking sheet into a 12- x 8-inch rectangle. Working with a long side, roll dough, jelly-roll style; pinch seam to seal (do not seal ends). Cut roll into 12 equal slices. Place slices, cut sides up, in muffin cups coated with cooking spray. Lightly coat tops of dough slices with melted butter. Cover; let rise in a warm place (85°F), free of drafts, 45 minutes or until doubled in size.

5. Preheat oven to 375°F. Bake rolls 15 to 20 minutes or until golden brown. Remove from pan, and cool 5 minutes on a wire rack. Serve rolls warm.

CHOCOLATEY CHRISTMAS PUDDING PIE

ACTIVE 20 MIN. • TOTAL 4 HOURS, 45 MIN. • SERVES 10

Melted chocolate binds cookie crumbs for the crust and makes it extra delicious. Red currants or raspberries may be substituted for the pomegranate seeds in the garnish. Dust with the powdered sugar just before serving, as it will dissolve quickly into the pudding top.

CRUST

1 (9-oz.) pkg. chocolate cookies (such Dewey's Brownie Crisps)

3 oz. bittersweet chocolate, melted

1 Tbsp. canola oil

FILLING

¾ cup sugar

¼ cup cornstarch

¼ cup unsweetened cocoa powder

¼ tsp. salt

1¾ cups whole milk, divided

2 large egg yolks

4 oz. bittersweet chocolate, finely chopped

1 Tbsp. white rum

Fresh mint leaves

¼ cup pomegranate seeds

Powdered sugar, for dusting (optional)

1. To prepare crust, place cookies in a food processor; process until finely ground. Add melted chocolate and oil; process until blended. Press into bottom and up sides of a 9-inch pie plate. Freeze 15 minutes or until set.

2. To prepare filling, combine sugar, cornstarch, cocoa, and salt in a large saucepan; stir with a whisk. Add half of the milk and the 2 egg yolks; stir with a whisk until smooth. Stir in remaining milk. Cook over medium heat for 5 minutes or until thick and bubbly, stirring constantly. Remove from heat. Add chopped chocolate, and stir until smooth. Stir in rum. Pour filling into prepared crust. Cover with plastic wrap; chill 4 hours or until set. Arrange pomegranate seeds and mint leaves in clusters to look like holly. Just before serving, dust with powdered sugar, if desired.

CLASSIC CHRISTMAS SUPPER

menu

Poinsettia Cocktail
Cherry-Pistachio Baked Brie
Greens-and-Grapes Salad
Cheesy Olive Rolls
Skillet Potato-Fennel Bake
Lemon-Garlic Green Beans
Sherry-Dijon Beef Tenderloin
Black Forest Cherry Cake

This menu of timeless recipe-box favorites transports taste buds down memory lane with flavors you crave, recipes to cook together, and dishes that will have guests begging for second helpings. Pass out the aprons, queue up the carols, and start the holiday celebration.

POINSETTIA COCKTAIL

ACTIVE **5 MIN.**

TOTAL **5 MIN.** • SERVES **1**

This sparkling ruby cocktail is like Christmas in a glass. It's easily modified to make it a mocktail.

Frozen cranberry

1 Tbsp. (½ oz.) Grand Marnier

6 Tbsp. (3 oz.) cranberry juice cocktail

6 Tbsp. (3 oz.) sparkling white wine, such as Champagne, prosecco, or Cava

Fresh rosemary sprig

Drop frozen cranberry into a chilled champagne flute and add Grand Marnier and cranberry juice. Pour in sparkling wine and garnish with rosemary sprig.

Make It a Mocktail:

Substitute orange juice for the Grand Marnier and sparkling grape juice or club soda for the sparkling wine.

CHERRY-PISTACHIO BAKED BRIE

ACTIVE **10 MIN.**

TOTAL **15 MIN.** • SERVES **8**

You can have this festive, easy appetizer ready in less than 30 minutes.

1 (16-oz.) round Brie cheese

½ cup cherry preserves

1 Tbsp. balsamic vinegar

⅛ tsp. salt

⅛ tsp. freshly ground black pepper

Chopped toasted shelled pistachios

Crackers

1. Preheat oven to 350°F. Line a small baking sheet with parchment paper or aluminum foil. Unwrap cheese; remove and discard rind from top and discard. Place Brie on prepared baking sheet. Bake until cheese is just warm and slightly soft to the touch, 5 to 7 minutes.

2. Stir together cherry preserves, balsamic vinegar, salt, and pepper, and salt in a bowl. Drizzle over warm Brie round and top with pistachios. Serve with crackers.

GREENS-AND-GRAPES SALAD

ACTIVE **15 MIN.**

TOTAL **15 MIN.** • SERVES **8**

Manchego cheese has a firm texture with a nutty, buttery, mildly sharp flavor that's easy to like. Use a vegetable peeler to shave cheese into big pieces.

¾ cup olive oil

¼ cup red wine vinegar

1½ Tbsp. Dijon mustard

1½ tsp. honey

⅛ tsp. salt

⅛ tsp. black pepper

1 (5-oz.) pkg. spring greens mix or sweet baby greens

2 cups seedless red grapes, halved

1 cup salted roasted cashews

2 oz. Manchego cheese, shaved

Stir together first 6 ingredients in a large serving bowl. Add greens and remaining ingredients, and toss. Serve immediately.

CHEESY OLIVE ROLLS

ACTIVE **10 MIN.**

TOTAL **25 MIN.** • SERVES **8 TO 10**

Though similar, Asiago cheese has a sweeter flavor than Parmesan or Romano. Store-bought tapenade is an easy cheat that cuts down on prep without sacrificing flavor.

1 (13.8-oz.) can refrigerated classic pizza crust dough

¼ cup prepared olive tapenade

½ cup grated Asiago cheese

1 tsp. chopped fresh rosemary

1 Tbsp. butter, melted

Preheat oven to 450°F. Unroll pizza crust dough. Spread olive tapenade over dough, leaving a ¼-inch border. Sprinkle with cheese and rosemary. Gently roll up dough, starting at one long side. Cut into 10 (1¼-inch-thick) slices. Place slices in a lightly greased 9-inch round cake pan. Brush top of dough with melted butter. Bake 12 to 15 minutes or until tops are golden brown. Serve immediately.

SKILLET POTATO-FENNEL BAKE

ACTIVE **15 MIN.**

TOTAL **1 HOUR, 5 MIN.** • SERVES **8**

Fennel adds its distinctive sweetness to this simple potato dish.

1 fennel bulb

3 Tbsp. olive oil

2 lb. red potatoes, thinly sliced

2 tsp. chopped fresh thyme

1½ tsp. salt

½ tsp. black pepper

Fresh fennel fronds

1. Preheat oven to 475°F. Rinse fennel thoroughly. Trim and discard root end of fennel bulb. Trim stalks from bulb, reserving fronds for garnish. Thinly slice bulb.

2. Add oil to a 9-inch cast-iron skillet. Arrange half of potato slices in skillet. Layer with fennel slices and remaining potatoes. Sprinkle with thyme, salt, and pepper. Cover with aluminum foil.

3. Bake at 475°F for 35 minutes. Uncover; bake 15 more minutes or until vegetables are browned. Serve hot or at room temperature. If desired, transfer to serving bowl. Garnish with fennel fronds.

LEMON-GARLIC GREEN BEANS

ACTIVE **15 MIN.**

TOTAL **20 MIN.** • SERVES **8**

1½ lb. fresh haricots verts (tiny green beans), trimmed

2 tsp. salt, divided

3 garlic cloves, minced

3 shallots, sliced

2 Tbsp. olive oil

¼ cup chopped fresh basil

3 Tbsp. fresh lemon juice

¼ tsp. black pepper

Garnishes: lemon zest, fresh basil leaves

1. Cook beans with 1 tsp. salt in boiling water to cover 4 to 5 minutes or until crisp-tender; drain. Plunge beans into ice water to stop the cooking process; drain.

2. Cook garlic and shallots in hot oil in a large skillet over medium heat 2 minutes or until just golden brown; remove from heat. Stir in chopped basil, lemon juice, pepper, and remaining 1 tsp. salt. Add green beans, and toss to coat. Garnish, if desired.

SHERRY-DIJON BEEF TENDERLOIN

ACTIVE **40 MIN.** · TOTAL **40 MIN.** · SERVES **8**

As simple as this dish is to make, it looks and tastes like a special-occasion meal. Ask your butcher for the Chateaubriand cut, which is an evenly sized portion taken from the center of the tenderloin.

---

1 (4-lb.) beef tenderloin, trimmed

4½ Tbsp. olive oil, divided

3 tsp. kosher salt, divided

3 tsp. black pepper, divided

½ cup minced shallots

2 large fresh thyme sprigs

1 cup dry sherry

6 cups unsalted beef stock

4 Tbsp. unsalted butter

4 Tbsp. torn fresh flat-leaf parsley

2 Tbsp. Dijon mustard

1. Preheat oven to 500°F. Place tenderloin in a roasting pan; rub with 1½ Tbsp. oil. Sprinkle tenderloin with 2½ tsp. salt and 2½ tsp. pepper.

2. Place in oven and immediately reduce heat to 400°F. Roast until a thermometer inserted in thickest portion registers 130°F for rare or 140°F for medium-rare, 10 to 15 minutes. Remove from oven; let stand 10 minutes before slicing.

3. Add shallots and thyme to a large saucepan. Cook over medium-high, stirring often, until lightly browned, 1 to 2 minutes. Add sherry. Bring to a boil; simmer until reduced by half, 2 to 3 minutes. Add stock, and bring to a boil; boil, stirring occasionally, until slightly syrupy and reduced to 1⅓ cups, about 15 minutes. Remove from heat. Stir in butter, parsley, mustard, remaining 3 Tbsp. oil, remaining ½ tsp. salt, and remaining ½ tsp. pepper; stir until butter melts.

4. Thinly slice beef; serve with sauce.

BLACK FOREST CHERRY CAKE

ACTIVE **40 MIN.** • TOTAL **1 HOUR, 25 MIN.** • SERVES **16**

The heavy cherry filling may cause the cake to sink slightly in the center once assembled, but it won't detract from the stunning presentation, which is easier to prepare than it appears. Canned or jarred Montmorency cherries in water have a more vibrant crimson color than most varieties in local supermarkets. It's worth the time to check out specialty grocery stores or to order them online for this impressive dessert.

FILLING

⅔ cup sugar

⅔ cup cranberry juice cocktail

¼ cup water

3 Tbsp. cornstarch

2 (14.5-oz.) cans pitted tart cherries in water, drained

CAKE

7.75 oz. all-purpose flour (about 1¾ cups)

2 cups sugar

¾ cup unsweetened cocoa powder

2 tsp. baking soda

1 tsp. baking powder

¼ tsp. salt

1 cup nonfat buttermilk

1 cup fat-free milk

¼ cup canola oil

1 tsp. vanilla extract

2 large eggs

Cooking spray

2 cups frozen whipped topping, thawed

1 Tbsp. kirsch (cherry brandy)

½ oz. dark chocolate curls

Powdered sugar, for dusting (optional)

1. To prepare filling, combine first 4 ingredients in a large saucepan; stir until cornstarch dissolves. Heat pan over medium-high heat; bring to a boil, stirring constantly. Cook 1 minute or until sugar mixture is very thick, stirring constantly. Remove sugar mixture from heat. Stir in cherries. Cool completely; cover and set aside.

2. To prepare cake, preheat oven to 350°F.

3. Weigh or lightly spoon flour into dry measuring cups; level with a knife. Combine flour and next 5 ingredients (through salt) in a large bowl; stir with a whisk. Combine buttermilk, milk, oil, vanilla, and eggs in a separate bowl; stir with a whisk. Add buttermilk mixture to sugar mixture; beat with a mixer at medium speed just until well blended (batter will be thin).

4. Pour batter into 2 (9-inch) round cake pans coated with cooking spray. Bake at 350°F for 40 minutes or until a wooden pick inserted in center comes out clean. Cool in pans 10 minutes; remove from pans. Cool completely on a wire rack.

5. Place 1 cake layer on a plate, and spoon half of cherry filling (about 1½ cups) evenly over the top, leaving a ¼-inch border around edges. Combine whipped topping and kirsch in a small bowl. Spoon 1 cup whipped topping mixture evenly over filling. Top with remaining cake layer. Spoon remaining 1½ cups filling onto cake layer, leaving a ½-inch border around edges. Spoon remaining 1 cup whipped topping mixture onto cherry mixture, leaving a 2-inch border from the edge of the cake layer. Garnish with chocolate curls. Cover loosely, and chill until ready to serve. Right before serving, dust with powdered sugar, if desired.

SAVOR & SHARE

HOLIDAY MENUS

MORNING JOYS

recipes

Double-Berry French Toast Casserole

Cardamom-Orange Rolls

Cheese Blintzes with Mixed Berry Topping

Red-and-Green Breakfast Parfaits

DOUBLE-BERRY FRENCH TOAST CASSEROLE

ACTIVE **40 MIN.** • TOTAL **9 HOURS, 30 MIN.**, **INCLUDING CHILLING** • SERVES **8**

2 (6-oz.) containers raspberries

1 (16-oz.) container strawberries

5 Tbsp. sugar, divided

2 Tbsp. berry liqueur, such as Chambord (optional)

10 oz. cream cheese, softened

12 oz. French baguette, cut into 16 round slices

1½ cups whole milk

½ tsp. ground cinnamon

½ tsp. vanilla extract

¼ tsp. salt

5 large eggs, lightly beaten

2 Tbsp. turbinado (raw) sugar

Maple syrup, warmed

Garnishes: sweetened whipped cream, fresh strawberries and raspberries

1. Combine raspberries, strawberries, 2 Tbsp. sugar, and the liqueur, if using, in a medium bowl; toss gently to coat. Let stand 30 minutes.

2. Strain berry liquid into a medium bowl, reserving berries. Add cream cheese to liquid, and stir to combine.

3. Spread cream mixture evenly over 1 side of 16 bread slices. Place 8 bread slices, cream cheese side up, in a 9- x 13-inch baking dish. Sprinkle with reserved strawberries and raspberries. Top with remaining 8 bread slices, cream cheese side down.

4. Whisk together milk, cinnamon, vanilla, salt, eggs, and remaining 3 Tbsp. sugar in a medium bowl; pour milk mixture evenly over bread slices, and sprinkle with turbinado sugar. Cover with foil, and refrigerate 8 hours or overnight.

5. Preheat oven to 350°F. Bake, uncovered, 50 minutes or until top is lightly browned and set. Serve with maple syrup; garnish, if desired.

CARDAMOM-ORANGE ROLLS

ACTIVE **25 MIN.** · TOTAL **2 HOURS, 30 MIN.** · SERVES **12**

Classic cinnamon rolls get a zingy update with exotic spice in this citrus-glazed twist.

1 (2¼-oz.) pkg. instant
  dry yeast

3 Tbsp. warm water (100°F to
  110°F)

10.13 oz. (about 2¼ cups) plus
  3 Tbsp. all-purpose flour,
  plus more for surface

½ tsp. salt

¼ cup granulated sugar

¼ cup whole milk

1¼ tsp. vanilla extract, divided

1 large egg

1 large egg yolk

5 Tbsp. unsalted butter,
  softened, divided

Cooking spray

⅓ cup packed brown sugar

1 Tbsp. grated orange zest,
  divided

1 tsp. ground cardamom

¾ cup powdered sugar

2 to 3 tsp. fresh orange juice

1. Combine yeast and 3 Tbsp. water in a small bowl; let stand 10 minutes or until foamy.

2. Lightly spoon flour into dry measuring cups; level with a knife. Combine flour and salt in a bowl; stir with a whisk to combine.

3. Place granulated sugar, milk, 1 tsp. vanilla, egg, and egg yolk in a large bowl. Beat with a mixer at medium-low speed until well combined. Stir in yeast mixture. Add half of the flour mixture; beat at low speed until well combined, about 2 minutes. Add remaining flour mixture; beat at low speed 5 minutes, occasionally scraping down sides of bowl. Add 4 Tbsp. of the butter, 1 tablespoon at a time, beating well after each addition. Dust a work surface with flour. Scrape dough onto work surface (dough will be sticky). Knead dough 3 to 4 minutes or until smooth and elastic. Shape dough into a ball. Place dough in a large bowl lightly coated with cooking spray, turning to coat surface. Cover and let rise in a warm place (85°F), free from drafts, for 2 hours.

4. Combine brown sugar, 1½ tsp. zest, and the cardamom in a small bowl. Turn dough out onto surface dusted with flour; gently pat dough into a 12- x 8-inch rectangle and brush with remaining 1 Tbsp. butter. Sprinkle evenly with brown sugar mixture. Beginning at one long side, roll up dough tightly, jelly-roll fashion; pinch seam to seal (do not seal ends of roll). Cut dough into 12 (1-inch) slices. Arrange slices in muffin cups coated with cooking spray. Cover with plastic wrap coated with cooking spray and let rise 45 minutes.

5. Preheat oven to 350°F.

6. Uncover rolls. Bake at 350°F for 15 minutes or until lightly browned. Cool 10 minutes in pan on a wire rack. Remove rolls from pan.

7. Combine powdered sugar, remaining ¼ tsp. vanilla, remaining 1½ tsp. zest, and 2 tsp. juice. Whisk until smooth. Add additional juice, a few drops at a time, if glaze is too stiff to spread. Spread glaze over warm rolls; serve warm.

TIP: Bake a Second Batch

Double the dough in a large bowl (it will fit in the bowl of a stand mixer); divide dough in half, and place in separate bowls to rise. If you don't have muffin tins to accommodate 24 rolls, bake one (12-roll) batch in an 8-inch square glass or ceramic baking dish, and increase the bake time to 20 to 23 minutes.

CHEESE BLINTZES WITH MIXED BERRY TOPPING

ACTIVE **15 MIN.** · TOTAL **15 MIN.** · SERVES **6**

Make the mixed berry topping while the filled crepes are baking in the oven; you don't have to thaw the berries first, so you can make the sauce quickly with any berries you have on hand, straight from the freezer.

¾ cup (6 oz.) cream cheese, softened

¾ cup ricotta cheese

3 Tbsp. brown sugar

6 (½-oz.) purchased crepes, halved

Cooking spray

Mixed Berry Topping (recipe follows)

Powdered sugar

1. Preheat oven to 450°F.

2. Place first 3 ingredients in a food processor; process until smooth. Spoon 6 Tbsp. cheese mixture down center of each crepe; fold sides and ends over filling. Place crepes, seam sides down, in a 13- x 9-inch baking dish coated with cooking spray. Coat crepes with cooking spray. Bake at 450°F for 5 minutes or until crepes are lightly browned.

3. While blintzes bake, prepare Mixed Berry Topping. Spoon topping evenly over blintzes. Dust with powdered sugar, if desired.

MIXED BERRY TOPPING

3 cups frozen mixed berries

2 Tbsp. honey

1½ tsp. grated lemon zest

2 Tbsp. chopped fresh mint

Combine the first 3 ingredients in a small saucepan. Cook over medium-high for 2 minutes or until thoroughly heated, stirring constantly. Remove from heat. Stir in mint. Makes a generous 2 cups

RED-AND-GREEN BREAKFAST PARFAITS

ACTIVE **15 MIN.** · TOTAL **1 HOUR** · SERVES **6**

Festive and filling, these pretty parfaits will help you kick-start your day with holiday flair.

6 kiwi fruits, peeled and each
  cut into 6 wedges

2 cups vanilla-flavor Greek
  yogurt

2 cups granola (without
  raisins)

½ cup honey

1 cup fresh raspberries

1½ Tbsp. chopped pistachios

Place 2 kiwi wedges in the bottom of each of 6 parfait glasses. Layer with about 2½ Tbsp. yogurt and about 2½ Tbsp. granola. Repeat layers once. Top each parfait with 2 more kiwi wedges, and drizzle each with a generous tablespoon of honey. Divide raspberries among glasses and sprinkle evenly with pistachios.

WARM STARTS

recipes

Chestnut Soup

Parsnip-and-Pear Soup

Shrimp Bisque

Hoppin' John Stew

CHESTNUT SOUP

ACTIVE **25 MIN.** • TOTAL **45 MIN.** • SERVES **6**

Chestnuts deliver silky richness and toasty flavor to this soul-warming holiday soup.

1 Tbsp. unsalted butter

1 cup chopped onion

½ cup chopped carrot

1½ cups peeled and steamed chestnuts (such as Melissa's)

2 tsp. chopped fresh thyme

½ tsp. ground ginger

¼ tsp. ground allspice

¼ cup apple brandy

2½ Tbsp. flour

3 cups chicken stock

½ tsp. kosher salt

1 Tbsp. apple cider vinegar

½ tsp. freshly ground black pepper

Heavy cream

Fresh thyme leaves

Grated nutmeg

1. Heat butter in a saucepan over medium heat. Add onion and carrot; cook 10 minutes. Stir in chestnuts, chopped thyme, ginger, and allspice; cook 1 minute. Add apple brandy; cook until reduced by half.

2. Whisk flour into chicken stock. Add stock mixture and 1 cup water to saucepan. Bring to a boil; reduce heat, cover, and simmer 12 minutes. Place mixture in a blender. Blend until smooth. Return to pan; cook over low heat 3 minutes. Stir in salt, vinegar, and pepper. Garnish with a drizzle of heavy cream, thyme leaves, and grated nutmeg.

PARSNIP-AND-PEAR SOUP

ACTIVE **15 MIN.** · TOTAL **7 HOURS, 15 MIN.** · SERVES **6 TO 8**

A parsnip is a creamy-white, carrot-shape root vegetable with a unique piquant, yet sweet flavor. Avoid parsnips that are limp or have brown spots.

1 Tbsp. olive oil

½ cup chopped onion

4 garlic cloves, minced

5 cups chicken broth

2 tsp. chopped fresh rosemary

½ tsp. salt

½ tsp. freshly ground black pepper

2 lb. parsnips, peeled and chopped

2 ripe pears, peeled and chopped

½ cup half-and-half

Garnishes: olive oil, cooked and crumbled bacon, fresh rosemary leaves

1. Heat oil in a large skillet over medium-high heat. Add onion and garlic; sauté 3 minutes or until tender.

2. Combine onion mixture, broth, and next 5 ingredients in a 4-qt. slow cooker. Cover and cook on HIGH for 7 hours.

3. Stir half-and-half into soup. Process soup, in batches, in a blender until smooth, stopping to scrape down sides as necessary. Pour soup into bowls. Garnish, if desired.

SHRIMP BISQUE

ACTIVE **30 MIN.** • TOTAL **40 MIN.** • SERVES **6**

You can easily swap out the shrimp for frozen peeled crawfish tails if you prefer.

6 Tbsp. salted butter

6 Tbsp. all-purpose flour

1 medium-size yellow onion, diced

1 red bell pepper, diced

2 celery stalks, diced

2 garlic cloves

1 medium tomato, diced

1½ tsp. kosher salt

½ tsp. black pepper

¼ tsp. cayenne pepper

3 cups seafood stock

4 fresh thyme sprigs

2 bay leaves

½ cup dry sherry cooking wine, divided

1 lb. frozen peeled shrimp, thawed and divided

½ cup heavy whipping cream

1 Tbsp. fresh lemon juice

1 tsp. hot sauce

2 Tbsp. chopped fresh chives

1. Melt butter in a saucepan over medium. Whisk in flour until combined. Reduce heat to medium-low, and cook, stirring constantly, until roux is pale brown, about 10 minutes. Add onion and next 7 ingredients, and cook, stirring occasionally, 5 minutes. Increase heat to medium-high. Whisk in stock, thyme, bay leaves, and ¼ cup cooking wine; cook 10 minutes. Add half of shrimp; cook 2 minutes. Remove thyme and bay leaves.

2. Transfer mixture to a blender, and process until smooth, 30 seconds. Return to pan, and place over medium-low heat. Stir in cream, lemon juice, hot sauce, remaining shrimp, and remaining ¼ cup cooking wine. Bring to a low simmer, and cook until heated, about 5 minutes. Spoon into bowls, and top with chives.

HOPPIN' JOHN STEW

ACTIVE **15 MIN.** • TOTAL **6 HOURS, 20 MIN.** • MAKES **18 CUPS**

Relying on prepared and canned ingredients means you can get this hearty, good-luck New Year's stew simmering in a slow cooker or on the stove in a flash. This recipe makes enough for a large crowd. Or enjoy a batch now and freeze the rest for later.

---

4 (15.8-oz.) cans black-eyed peas, undrained

2 (10-oz.) cans diced tomatoes and green chiles, undrained

1 (14-oz.) can beef broth

1 lb. smoked sausage, sliced

1 cup water

1 cup finely chopped onion

¾ cup chopped green bell pepper

½ tsp. garlic powder

¼ tsp. salt

¼ tsp. black pepper

1 family-size pkg. boil-in-bag rice, uncooked (about 1½ cups uncooked)

1. Combine all ingredients except rice in a 6-qt. slow cooker.

2. Cover and cook on LOW 6 hours. Cut top off boil-in-bag rice; pour rice into slow cooker, and discard bag. Stir.

3. Cover and cook on HIGH 20 minutes or until rice is tender.

. . . .

Save Some Soup!

Most leftover soups will last up to 3 days in the fridge or up to 1 month in the freezer. Just follow these easy steps.

1. Cool. Refrigerators and freezers cannot cool soups quickly enough to be food safe. Speed up the cooling process by placing the removable liner of your slow cooker in a bath of ice water in the sink. Make certain the slow cooker you own allows for this step. If you are uncertain, simply put the soup in a large pot or Dutch oven. Stir soup often to help release the heat.

2. Package. Plastic freezer containers work just fine but tend to take up precious space in your freezer. Instead, label and date gallon- or quart-size zip-top plastic freezer bags, place in a bowl, and cuff the bag over the rim. Ladle soup into each bag, and let out any excess air; seal.

3. Freeze. Lay bags flat in a single layer in the freezer; when frozen, stack bags.

4. Reheat. Thaw overnight in fridge. Thick soups like chowders should be reheated over low heat; reheat others over medium-low. Be sure to stir occasionally.

. . . .

SEASONAL SHOWSTOPPERS

recipes

Pork Tenderloins with Shaved Vegetables

Herb-Rubbed Smoked Turkey

Spiral-Cut Ham with Fig and Thyme Glaze

Salmon with Pecan-Dill Crust

PORK TENDERLOINS WITH SHAVED VEGETABLES

ACTIVE **25 MIN.** • TOTAL **25 MIN.** • SERVES **8**

*Use a sharp paring knife or a Y-shape peeler to thinly shave the carrots for the salad.
A mandoline works best on the radishes and fennel bulb.*

½ cup olive oil, divided

2 (1½-lb.) pork tenderloins, trimmed

4 tsp. kosher salt, divided

2 tsp. black pepper, divided

¼ cup fresh lemon juice (from 2 medium lemons)

2 small shallots, chopped (2 Tbsp.)

2 Tbsp. Dijon mustard

1 Tbsp. plus 1 tsp. honey

2 medium fennel bulbs, thinly shaved (4 cups)

4 large carrots, shaved (4 cups)

4 medium parsnips, thinly shaved (4 cups)

8 large radishes, thinly shaved (2 cups)

1 cup fresh flat-leaf parsley leaves, plus more for garnish

Fresh thyme sprigs

Fresh rosemary sprigs

1. Preheat oven to 400°F. Heat 2 Tbsp. oil in a large ovenproof skillet over medium-high. Sprinkle tenderloins with 3 tsp. salt and 1 tsp. pepper, and cook, turning occasionally, until well browned on all sides, about 8 minutes. Place skillet in oven, and bake until a thermometer inserted in thickest portion of tenderloins registers 140°F, about 10 minutes. Remove pork from skillet, and let stand 10 minutes.

2. Meanwhile, whisk together lemon juice, shallots, mustard, honey, and remaining 1 tsp. each salt and pepper in a large bowl. Whisk in remaining 6 Tbsp. oil until emulsified. Add fennel, carrots, radishes, parsnips, and parsley, and toss until evenly coated.

3. Thinly slice pork, and serve with vegetables. Garnish with additional parsley leaves, and thyme and rosemary sprigs, if desired.

HERB-RUBBED SMOKED TURKEY

ACTIVE **30 MIN.** • TOTAL **15 HOURS, 40 MIN.** • SERVES **10**

Start a new tradition that will free up your oven and result in a moist, juicy bird.

3 Tbsp. kosher salt

3 Tbsp. dark brown sugar

2 tsp. dried thyme

2 tsp. dried rosemary, chopped

2 tsp. dried sage

1½ tsp. black pepper

1 tsp. garlic powder

1 (12- to 14-lb.) whole fresh or frozen turkey, thawed

½ cup unsalted butter, softened

3 cups hickory chips

Three Rules for Smoked Turkey

BRINE, AND THEN BUTTER

For the most flavor, dry-brine the turkey with the rub, and refrigerate to dry the skin. Then add a layer of butter, mixed with more rub, under the skin.

DON'T SOAK THE CHIPS

Wet chips smolder over a long period of time, oversmoking the turkey. Dry chips burn instantly and die down as it cooks, giving the right amount of smoke.

PULL IT EARLY

Turkey is safe to eat when it reaches 165°F. Remove it from the smoker at 155°F, and tent with foil. It will continue to cook as it rests and will remain moist.

1. Stir together salt, brown sugar, thyme, rosemary, sage, pepper, and garlic powder in a small bowl; set aside herb rub.

2. Remove giblets and neck from turkey; reserve for another use. Pat turkey dry with paper towels. Reserve 1 Tbsp. herb rub for Step 3. Rub 1 Tbsp. herb rub inside cavity, and sprinkle outside of turkey with remaining amount; massage into skin. Chill, uncovered, 10 to 24 hours.

3. Stir together butter and reserved 1 Tbsp. herb rub. Loosen skin from turkey breast without totally detaching it; spread butter mixture under skin. Replace skin, securing with wooden picks if needed. Tie ends of legs together with kitchen twine, tuck wing tips under, and let stand at room temperature 30 minutes.

4. Prepare a charcoal fire in a smoker according to manufacturer's instructions, bringing internal temperature to 225 F to 235 F. Maintain temperature inside smoker 15 to 20 minutes. Place hickory chips on coals. Smoke turkey, breast side up, covered with smoker lid, until a thermometer inserted in thickest portion of turkey registers 155 F, 5 to 6 hours.

5. Remove turkey from smoker, cover loosely with heavy-duty aluminum foil, and let stand 20 minutes before slicing.

CAJUN SMOKED TURKEY

Stir together 3 Tbsp. kosher salt; 3 Tbsp. light brown sugar; 2 tsp. each paprika, dried oregano, and cayenne pepper; and 1 tsp. garlic powder in a small bowl to make Cajun rub. Prepare recipe as directed, substituting Cajun rub for herb rub.

SPIRAL-CUT HAM WITH FIG AND THYME GLAZE

ACTIVE **30 MIN.** • TOTAL **2 HOURS, 30 MIN.** • SERVES **15**

Rethink the holiday classic with a fruity new glaze.

1 (7- to 10-lb.) fully cooked bone-in spiral-cut half ham

Fig and Thyme Glaze (recipe follows)

Garnishes: whole and halved fresh figs, red grapes, and fresh thyme sprigs

1. Preheat oven to 350°F with oven rack in lower third position. Let ham stand at room temperature 30 minutes.

2. Line a roasting pan with aluminum foil, and place a rack in prepared pan; pour 3 cups water into bottom of pan. Place ham on rack, cut side down.

3. Bake at 350°F for 1 hour, 30 minutes, basting with pan drippings every 30 minutes. Add more water to roasting pan as needed if it evaporates.

4. Brush ham all over with half of glaze. Bake for 15 more minutes. Brush ham all over with remaining glaze, and bake until a thermometer inserted into thickest portion of ham registers 140°F, about 15 minutes. Remove from oven, and let stand 15 minutes. Transfer to a serving platter and garnish. Serve warm.

FIG AND THYME GLAZE

1 cup fig preserves
¼ cup apple cider vinegar
¼ cup honey
½ tsp. dried thyme
1 tsp. black pepper

Place all ingredients in a medium saucepan. Bring to a simmer, whisking occasionally, over medium-high heat, and simmer until well combined, 2 to 3 minutes. Reduce heat to low, and simmer until thickened and reduced by half, about 20 minutes. Remove from heat. Makes about ¾ cup

SALMON WITH PECAN-DILL CRUST

ACTIVE **10 MIN.** • TOTAL **30 MIN.** • SERVES **10 TO 12**

This refined whole side of salmon takes only 10 minutes to prep.

1½ cups pecan halves

6 Tbsp. butter, melted

2 garlic cloves, minced

1½ tsp. dried dill

1 (3- to 3½-lb.) boneless, skinless side of salmon

1¼ tsp. kosher salt

½ tsp. freshly ground black pepper

Garnishes: citrus halves and fresh dill sprigs

Preheat oven to 400°F. Pulse first 4 ingredients in a food processor 5 or 6 times or until mixture resembles coarse crumbs. Sprinkle salmon with salt and pepper; place on a parchment paper-lined baking sheet. Spread pecan mixture over salmon. Bake 18 to 20 minutes or just until salmon flakes with a fork. Transfer to a serving platter and garnish.

ALL THE TRIMMINGS

recipes

•———————•

Grated Sweet Potato Pudding with Pecans

Broccolini with Hollandaise Sauce

Creamy Baked Macaroni and Cheese with Bacon

Classic Cornbread Dressing

Spiked Cranberry-Orange Salad

GRATED SWEET POTATO PUDDING WITH PECANS

ACTIVE 20 MIN. • TOTAL 50 MIN. • SERVES 10

This creamy dish is accented beautifully by a topping of crunchy chopped pecans, arguably the South's favorite nut.

- ¼ cup unsalted butter
- 2 large eggs, well beaten
- ⅓ cup granulated sugar
- 2 Tbsp. all-purpose flour
- 2 tsp. kosher salt
- 1½ cups half-and-half
- 4 cups peeled, grated sweet potatoes (from 1½ lb. sweet potatoes)
- 1 cup chopped pecans

1. Preheat oven to 400°F. Melt butter in a deep 10-inch cast-iron skillet over medium-high. Remove from heat. Swirl to coat skillet with melted butter, then pour butter into a small bowl. Do not wipe skillet clean.

2. Stir together eggs, sugar, flour, and salt in a large bowl. Gradually add half-and-half, stirring constantly. Stir in melted butter until mixture is combined and smooth. Add sweet potatoes; stir to combine.

3. Transfer sweet potato mixture to buttered skillet; spread in an even layer. Arrange chopped pecans in a ring around edge of skillet. Bake at 400°F for 10 minutes. Reduce oven temperature to 350°F; continue baking until pudding is puffed up, firm, and nicely browned, 25 to 35 minutes. Serve hot or warm.

BROCCOLINI WITH HOLLANDAISE SAUCE

ACTIVE **25 MIN.** • TOTAL **25 MIN.** • SERVES **6 TO 8**

Serve this buttery sauce with green beans or asparagus too. The vegetables can be hot or at room temperature, but the sauce should be kept warm.

¼ cup kosher salt

3 bunches Broccolini, trimmed

½ cup salted butter

4 large pasteurized egg yolks

2 Tbsp. fresh lemon juice

½ tsp. kosher salt

⅛ tsp. ground white pepper

Dash of hot sauce (optional)

1. Bring salt and 8 qt. water to a boil in a large stockpot over high heat. Gently stir in Broccolini, and cook 3 to 4 minutes or until tender. Drain and pat dry. Arrange on a platter.

2. Melt butter in a small saucepan over medium heat; reduce heat to low, and keep warm. Process egg yolks, next 3 ingredients, 1 Tbsp. water, and, if desired, hot sauce in a blender or food processor 2 to 3 minutes or until pale and fluffy. With blender running, add melted butter in a slow stream, processing until smooth. Serve warm with Broccolini.

CREAMY BAKED MACARONI AND CHEESE WITH BACON

ACTIVE 30 MIN. • TOTAL 1 HOUR, 10 MIN. • SERVES 10

*Our take on this classic is familiar enough for the traditionalists but revved up just enough
to please those eager for something unexpected.*

---

1 lb. uncooked large elbow macaroni

1 Tbsp. plus 1½ tsp. kosher salt, divided

¾ cup fresh breadcrumbs

2 oz. Parmesan cheese, shredded or grated (about ½ cup)

6 thick-cut bacon slices, cooked and crumbled, divided

⅓ cup all-purpose flour

1 tsp. black pepper

1 tsp. dry mustard

3 cups whole milk

1 cup whole buttermilk

⅓ cup unsalted butter, plus more for greasing dish

12 oz. extra-sharp Cheddar cheese, shredded (about 3 cups)

4 oz. Monterey Jack, provolone, or mozzarella cheese, shredded (about 1 cup)

2 large eggs, well beaten

1. Preheat oven to 350°F. Bring 3 qt. water to a boil over high in a large stockpot. Stir in pasta and 1 Tbsp. salt, and return to a boil. Cook, stirring occasionally, until pasta is tender but still firm, about 6 minutes. Reserve and set aside 2 cups cooking water, and then drain the pasta. Return pasta to pot, and remove from heat. Cover to keep warm.

2. Generously butter a 13- x 9-inch baking dish, and set aside. Toss together breadcrumbs, Parmesan cheese, and half of the bacon in a bowl, and set aside. Stir together flour, pepper, mustard, and remaining 1½ tsp. salt in a small bowl. Heat milk and buttermilk in a medium saucepan over medium, undisturbed, until barely steaming but not boiling, 4 to 5 minutes. Set aside.

3. Melt butter in a large heavy saucepan over medium-high. Add flour mixture. Cook, whisking often, until mixture is smooth and thick and has a delicate golden color and toasted aroma, about 2 minutes. Slowly whisk in warm milk mixture. Bring to a boil over high. Cook, stirring often, until thickened to the texture of cream, about 3 minutes.

4. Stir Cheddar and Monterey Jack cheeses into milk mixture, and remove from heat. Stir in eggs until mixture forms a smooth sauce.

5. Uncover cooked pasta, and stir. (If pasta sticks together, stir in reserved warm cooking water, and drain again.) Stir cheese mixture and remaining bacon into drained pasta in stockpot.

6. Transfer pasta mixture to prepared baking dish, and sprinkle evenly with breadcrumb mixture. Bake at 350°F until firm, puffed up, and lightly browned, 35 to 40 minutes. Serve hot or warm.

CLASSIC CORNBREAD DRESSING

ACTIVE **40 MIN.** • TOTAL **3 HOURS** • SERVES **15**

A great Southern-style dressing starts with cornbread that's baked in a skillet for a crisp, golden crust. Our simple recipe can be made up to a month ahead if stored in the freezer. For best results, prepare the cornbread up to two days in advance so it can dry out completely.

CORNBREAD

2 cups self-rising white cornmeal mix

1 tsp. granulated sugar (optional)

2 large eggs

2 cups whole buttermilk

3 Tbsp. salted butter

DRESSING

½ cup salted butter

3 cups chopped sweet onions (from 2 large onions)

2 cups chopped celery (from 6 stalks)

2 Tbsp. chopped fresh sage

1 tsp. chopped fresh thyme

6 large eggs

1 (14-oz.) pkg. herb-seasoned stuffing mix (such as Pepperidge Farm)

10 cups chicken broth

2 tsp. black pepper

1 tsp. kosher salt

1. Prepare the Cornbread: Preheat oven to 425°F. Combine self-rising cornmeal mix and, if desired, sugar in a large bowl. Stir together eggs and buttermilk in a medium bowl; add to cornmeal mixture, stirring just until moistened.

2. Heat butter in a 10-inch cast-iron skillet in preheated oven 5 minutes. Stir melted butter into batter. Pour batter into hot skillet.

3. Bake at 425°F until golden, about 25 minutes; cool in skillet 20 minutes. Remove from skillet to a wire rack, and cool completely, 20 to 30 more minutes. Crumble Cornbread. Freeze in a large heavy-duty zip-top plastic bag up to 1 month, if desired. Thaw in refrigerator.

4. Prepare the Dressing: Preheat oven to 350°F. Melt butter in a large skillet over medium-high; add onions and celery, and cook, stirring often, until tender, 10 to 12 minutes. Add sage and thyme, and cook, stirring often, 1 minute.

5. Stir together eggs in a very large bowl; stir in crumbled Cornbread, onion mixture, stuffing mix, chicken broth, pepper, and salt until blended.

6. Spoon Dressing mixture into 2 lightly greased 13- x 9-inch (3-qt.) baking dishes. Cover tightly and freeze up to 3 months, if desired; thaw in refrigerator 24 hours. (Uncover and let stand at room temperature 30 minutes before baking.)

7. Bake, uncovered, at 350°F until light golden brown and cooked through, 1 hour to 1 hour and 15 minutes.

Variations

PECAN-HERB CORNBREAD DRESSING

Prepare recipe as directed, increasing fresh thyme to 2 tsp. and adding 2 tsp. chopped fresh rosemary with herbs in Step 4. Stir 1½ cups chopped toasted pecans and ½ cup chopped fresh flat-leaf parsley into Cornbread mixture in Step 5; proceed as directed. Garnish with additional chopped parsley.

CORNBREAD DRESSING WITH SMOKED SAUSAGE AND APPLES

Cook 12 oz. chopped smoked sausage in a large skillet until cooked through. Transfer to a paper towel to drain; wipe skillet clean. Prepare recipe as directed, adding 2 large unpeeled Braeburn or Fuji apples, chopped (about 9 oz.), to onion mixture during the last 5 minutes of cook time in Step 4 before adding herbs. Stir sausage into Cornbread mixture in Step 5; proceed as directed.

SPIKED CRANBERRY-ORANGE SALAD

ACTIVE 25 MIN. · TOTAL 4 HOURS, 55 MIN. · SERVES 12

This can be made 3 days in advance. Cover and store in the refrigerator.

- **4 cups fresh or frozen cranberries (14 oz.)**
- **¾ cup packed light brown sugar**
- **½ cup fresh orange juice (from 2 oranges)**
- **1 cup clementine segments (about 4 clementines)**
- **2 Tbsp. orange-flavor liqueur**
- **1 Tbsp. orange zest (from 1 orange)**
- **1 cup chopped fresh pineapple (from 1 pineapple)**
- **½ cup thinly sliced celery (from 2 stalks)**
- **½ cup chopped toasted walnuts**

Bring cranberries, brown sugar, and orange juice to a boil in a large saucepan over medium-high, stirring often. Reduce heat to medium-low, and simmer, stirring occasionally, until cranberries pop and mixture thickens, 12 to 15 minutes. Remove from heat, and cool to room temperature, about 30 minutes. Stir in liqueur, orange zest, clementines, pineapple, celery, and walnuts. Transfer to a serving bowl; cover and chill salad 4 to 24 hours.

SAVE ROOM

recipes

Red Velvet-White Chocolate Cake

Frozen Peppermint Cheesecake

Rich Chocolate Pudding

Caramel-Sauced Apples

RED VELVET-WHITE CHOCOLATE CAKE

ACTIVE 50 MIN. • TOTAL 1 HOUR, 45 MIN., PLUS 55 MIN. COOLING • SERVES 12

Our classic Southern cover cake calls for a rich cream cheese frosting, and our recipe delivers with extra sweetness from white chocolate. Even if you skip the ruffled design, our Test Kitchen says this dessert will steal the show. Keep the frosting cool because it can soften and melt.

1 (15¼-oz.) pkg. red velvet cake mix (plus ingredients listed on box for preparing cake)

Baking spray with flour

1 cup unsalted butter, softened

1 (8-oz.) pkg. cream cheese, softened

5 cups unsifted powdered sugar

5 oz. white chocolate, melted and cooled slightly

1 tsp. vanilla extract

Assorted sizes of white, pink, and red sugar pearls (optional)

1. Preheat oven to 350°F. Prepare red velvet cake mix according to package directions. Divide batter evenly among 3 (6-inch) round cake pans coated with baking spray.

2. Bake at 350°F until a wooden pick inserted in centers of cakes comes out clean, 20 to 23 minutes. Cool in pans 10 minutes. Invert cakes onto wire racks; cool completely, about 45 minutes.

3. Beat softened butter and cream cheese with a stand mixer fitted with a paddle attachment on medium speed until smooth, about 2 minutes. With mixer on low speed, gradually add powdered sugar, white chocolate, and vanilla. Increase speed to medium-high; beat until fluffy, about 2 minutes. (You will have about 7 cups frosting.)

4. Place a cake plate on a lazy Susan or stand. Put 1 cake layer on plate; spread top with 1 cup frosting. Repeat with remaining 2 cake layers and 2 cups of the frosting. Using a large offset spatula, spread a thin layer of frosting (about 2 cups) over sides and top of entire cake. Remove cake plate with cake from lazy Susan, and chill until frosting is firm and set, about 30 minutes. Place about half of the remaining frosting (about 1 cup) in a piping bag fitted with a Wilton 1M star tip; set aside.

5. Return cake plate with cake to lazy Susan. Use remaining frosting to pipe small (about 1-inch) kisses side by side on top of cake. If desired, decorate with sugar pearls.

FROZEN PEPPERMINT CHEESECAKE

ACTIVE **25 MIN.** • TOTAL **4 HOURS, 40 MIN.** • SERVES **10**

Peppermint ice cream lovers, this one's for you!

40 vanilla wafers, finely crushed

¼ cup powdered sugar

¼ cup melted butter

1 (8-oz.) pkg. cream cheese, softened

1 (14-oz.) can sweetened condensed milk

1 cup crushed hard peppermint candies

3 drops red liquid food coloring

1 (8-oz.) container frozen whipped topping, thawed, divided

Garnish: crushed hard peppermint candies

1. Stir together crushed vanilla wafers, powdered sugar, and melted butter; firmly press onto bottom and 1 inch up the sides of a 9-inch springform pan. Freeze 15 minutes.

2. Beat cream cheese at high speed with an electric mixer until creamy. Stir in condensed milk, crushed candies, and food coloring. Fold in 2 cups whipped topping.

3. Pour cream cheese mixture into prepared crust; cover and freeze 4 hours or until firm. Spread remaining 1 cup whipped topping over cheesecake. Garnish, if desired.

RICH CHOCOLATE PUDDING

ACTIVE 5 MIN. • TOTAL 25 MIN. • SERVES 8

Boasting an intense flavor and a made-from-scratch taste, this simple chocolate pudding is a delicious any-night dessert. Placing plastic wrap on the surface of the hot pudding prevents a skin from forming during chilling.

---

1 (5-oz.) pkg. chocolate cook-and-serve pudding mix

1 large egg yolk

4 cups chocolate milk

1 oz. semisweet chocolate, chopped

1 tsp. vanilla extract

Whipped cream

Semisweet chocolate shavings

1. Combine first 3 ingredients in a medium saucepan. Bring to a boil over medium heat, stirring constantly with a whisk. Boil 2 minutes, stirring constantly. Remove from heat. Add chopped chocolate and vanilla, stirring with a whisk until chocolate melts. Cool 5 minutes.

2. Spoon ½ cup pudding into each of 8 individual serving bowls. Serve warm, or cover surface of pudding with plastic wrap, and chill thoroughly. Top each serving with whipped cream and a sprinkle with chocolate shavings.

CARAMEL-SAUCED APPLES

ACTIVE **10 MIN.** • TOTAL **45 MIN.** • SERVES **4**

This no-fuss treat comes together in minutes. The sauce, made of butter, apple juice, and a homemade caramel sauce, reduces while the apples bake, creating a velvety glaze. Make extra sauce, and store it in the refrigerator to serve over pound cake or ice cream for another quick dessert.

4 Granny Smith apples, peeled and cored

⅔ cup apple juice

2 Tbsp. butter, melted

Caramel Sauce (recipe follows)

Sugared Rosemary (recipe follows)

1. Preheat oven to 375°F.

2. Cut each apple horizontally into 5 slices. Reassemble each apple, and place in an 11- x 7-inch baking dish. Combine apple juice and melted butter; pour over apples. Bake at 375°F for 45 minutes or until apples are tender, basting with juices every 15 minutes.

3. Place an apple stack on each of 4 individual serving plates. Pour ¼ cup Caramel Sauce into center of each stack, allowing sauce to flow over sides. Garnish with Sugared Rosemary. Serve immediately.

CARAMEL SAUCE

1 cup sugar

⅓ cup water

1 Tbsp. butter

½ cup evaporated milk

½ tsp. vanilla extract

1. Combine sugar and water in a large skillet. Cook over medium heat 15 minutes or until golden (do not stir). Brush crystals from sides of pan with a wet pastry brush, if necessary.

2. Remove pan from heat; let stand 1 minute. Carefully add butter, stirring until butter melts. Gradually add milk, stirring constantly. (Caramel will harden and stick to spoon.) Cook over medium heat 2 minutes or until caramel melts and mixture is smooth and slightly thickened, stirring constantly. Remove from heat; stir in vanilla. Makes 1 cup.

SUGARED ROSEMARY

Brush 4 fresh rosemary sprigs with simple syrup or light corn syrup to thinly coat. Sprinkle sprigs generously all over with about ⅓ cup superfine sugar. Let dry about 1 hour.

BAKE IT FORWARD!

recipes

Merry Cherry Rugelach

Fudgy Chocolate-Peppermint Cookies

Chameleon Icebox Cookies with Variations

Caramel Tartlets

MERRY CHERRY RUGELACH

ACTIVE **20 MIN.**

TOTAL **1 HOUR, 25 MIN.** • MAKES **16**

You can switch out the cherry preserves and dried cherries for another fruit that comes in both spread and dried form, such as apricot, currant, or blueberry.

1 cup (about 5½ oz.) all-purpose flour

½ cup toasted, salted pecans, finely ground

¼ tsp. salt

6 Tbsp. unsalted butter, softened

3 Tbsp. granulated sugar

4 oz. cream cheese

½ tsp. vanilla extract

½ cup cherry fruit spread (such as Simply Fruit), divided

⅓ cup dried tart cherries, finely chopped and divided

2 Tbsp. whole milk

1½ Tbsp. turbinado sugar

1. Weigh or lightly spoon flour into a dry measuring cup; level with a knife. Combine flour, ground pecans, and salt in a bowl; stir with a whisk.

2. Place butter, sugar, and cream cheese in a large bowl; beat with a mixer at medium speed until well combined (about 5 minutes). Beat in vanilla. Add flour mixture; beat just until combined. Turn dough out onto a work surface; divide in half. Shape each portion into a disk; wrap each in plastic wrap. Chill 30 minutes.

3. Preheat oven to 350°F.

4. Place 1 dough disk on a lightly floured work surface. Roll dough into a 10-inch circle. Spread ¼ cup fruit spread over dough. Sprinkle half of dried cherries over top. Cut circle into 8 wedges, as you would a pizza. Beginning with long side, roll up each wedge. Place rolls, point sides down, 2 inches apart on a baking sheet lined with parchment paper. Repeat procedure with remaining dough disk, fruit spread, and dried cherries.

5. Brush dough with milk; sprinkle with turbinado sugar. Bake at 350°F for 22 minutes or until golden brown. Cool completely.

TIP: Bake a Second Batch
You can easily accommodate a double batch of dough in a large bowl. Divide into fourths, shaping each into a disk. Work with one portion at a time as you shape the cookies, and keep the rest chilled until you're ready for them.

FUDGY CHOCOLATE-PEPPERMINT COOKIES

ACTIVE **20 MIN.**

TOTAL **40 MIN.** • MAKES **2 DOZEN**

When a soft, fudgy cookie meets crunchy candy cane shards, it's a match made in heaven.

1½ cups (about 6.75 oz.) all-purpose flour

5 Tbsp. unsweetened cocoa powder, sifted

½ tsp. baking powder

¼ tsp. baking soda

¼ tsp. salt

1 cup sugar

8 Tbsp. unsalted butter, softened

¼ tsp. vanilla extract

1 large egg

3 Tbsp. crushed peppermint candy

1. Preheat oven to 350°F.

2. Weigh or lightly spoon flour into dry measuring cups; level with a knife. Combine flour, cocoa, baking powder, baking soda, and salt in a bowl, stirring with a whisk.

3. Place sugar and butter in a bowl. Beat with a mixer at medium speed until well combined (about 3 minutes). Add vanilla and egg, beating until well combined. Add flour mixture; beat at low speed just until combined.

4. Shape dough into 24 balls; place 2 inches apart on 2 baking sheets lined with parchment paper. Flatten cookies with the bottom of a glass. Mound a generous ¼ teaspoon crushed candy in center of each cookie. Bake at 350°F for 7 minutes. Cool completely on pans.

CHAMELEON ICEBOX COOKIES

ACTIVE 20 MIN. · TOTAL 1 HOUR, 40 MIN. · MAKES ABOUT 4 DOZEN

Old-fashioned icebox cookies become a creative and tasty blank canvas for Christmas stir-ins. You will be hard-pressed to choose a favorite variation.

---

1 cup butter, softened

1 cup superfine sugar

1 large egg

2 tsp. vanilla extract

2¼ cups (about 9⅝ oz.) all-purpose flour

½ tsp. salt

1. Beat butter at medium speed with an electric mixer until creamy; gradually add sugar, beating well. Add egg and vanilla; beat well.

2. Combine flour and salt; add to butter mixture, beating at medium-low speed just until blended. Cover and chill dough at least 1 hour.

3. Shape dough into 2 (6-inch) logs. Wrap logs in wax paper or parchment paper; chill or freeze until firm.

4. Preheat oven to 350°F. Slice dough into ¼-inch-thick slices. Place on ungreased baking sheets. Bake at 350°F for 12 minutes or until barely golden. Remove to wire racks, and let cool completely (about 10 minutes).

Variations

SHIMMERING CHOCOLATE-ORANGE ESSENCE ICEBOX COOKIES

Stir ½ cup (4 oz.) finely chopped bittersweet chocolate and 1 Tbsp. orange zest into dough. Roll 1 log in ⅓ cup gold sanding sugar. Roll remaining log in ⅓ cup sparkling sanding sugar. Proceed with recipe as directed.

STRAWBERRY-PISTACHIO ICEBOX COOKIES

Stir ¾ cup finely chopped dried strawberries into dough. Roll logs in 1 cup finely chopped pistachios. Proceed with recipe as directed.

CHRISTMAS COLORS ICEBOX COOKIES

Roll 1 log of dough in ⅓ cup red nonpareils. Roll remaining log in ⅓ cup green nonpareils. Proceed with recipe as directed.

LAVENDER ICEBOX COOKIES

Stir 1½ Tbsp. dried lavender, lightly crushed, into dough. Proceed with recipe as directed.

CARAMEL TARTLETS

ACTIVE **30 MIN.** · TOTAL **4 HOURS, 30 MIN., INCLUDING PASTRY SHELLS** · MAKES **6 DOZEN**

Add a festive touch! Just before serving, sprinkle tarts with finely chopped chocolate, crystallized ginger, toffee, sea salt, or toasted pecans.

---

2 cups sugar, divided

½ cup cold butter, sliced

6 Tbsp. all-purpose flour

4 large egg yolks

2 cups milk

Cream Cheese Pastry Shells (recipe follows)

1. Cook 1 cup sugar in a medium-size heavy skillet over medium heat, stirring constantly, 6 to 8 minutes or until sugar melts and turns golden brown. Stir in butter until melted.

2. Whisk together flour, egg yolks, milk, and remaining 1 cup sugar in a 3-qt. heavy saucepan; bring just to a simmer over low heat, whisking constantly. Add sugar mixture to flour mixture, and cook, whisking constantly, 1 to 2 minutes or until thickened. Cover and chill 4 hours.

3. Meanwhile, prepare Cream Cheese Pastry Shells. Spoon caramel mixture into pastry shells, and garnish as desired.

CREAM CHEESE PASTRY SHELLS

1 cup butter, softened

1 (8-oz.) pkg. cream cheese, softened

3½ cups all-purpose flour

1. Beat butter and cream cheese at medium speed with a heavy-duty electric stand mixer until creamy. Gradually add flour to butter mixture, beating at low speed just until blended. Shape dough into 72 (¾-inch) balls, and place on a baking sheet; cover and chill 1 hour.

2. Preheat oven to 400°F. Place dough balls in cups of lightly greased miniature muffin pans; press dough to top of cups, forming shells.

3. Bake at 400°F for 10 to 12 minutes. Remove from pans to wire racks, and cool completely (about 15 minutes). Makes 6 dozen

TIP: Baked pastry shells may be made up to one month ahead and frozen in an airtight container. Thaw at room temperature before filling.

THANKS

Thanks to the following shops, vendors, and artisans whose products were featured on the pages of this book and to the many more not listed here:

Accent Décor

ALKMY

A'mano

At Home Furnishings

BC Clark

Bebe's

Bromberg's

Buzz

Christmas Expressions

Davis Wholesale Florist

Estelle

Etsy

Hall's Birmingham
Wholesale Florist

Hobby Lobby

House and Parties

John Derian Company

Leaf & Petal

Lion Ribbon

Me Home

Merry by Julie Terrell

Molly Mahon

Oak Street Garden Shop

OKC Wholesale
Flower Market

Park Hill Collection

Pastiche Studios

Riley Sheehey

Scissortail Marketplace

Sexton's Seafood

Shoppe

Son of a Butcher

Target

Terrain

Trader Joe's

Vietri

Whole Foods

XO by Haileigh Kenney

Thanks to the following individuals and venues for allowing us into their homes to decorate and photograph.

Sara Gae and Greg Waters

Maggie and Blair Humphreys

Carter and Fred Fellers

General Index

Metric Charts

The recipes that appear in this cookbook use the standard US method for measuring liquid and dry or solid ingredients (teaspoons, tablespoons, and cups). The information on these pages is provided to help cooks outside the United States successfully use these recipes. All equivalents are approximate.

Metric Equivalents for Different Types of Ingredients

A standard cup measure of a dry or solid ingredient will vary in weight depending on the type of ingredient. A standard cup of liquid is the same volume for any type of liquid. Use the following chart when converting standard cup measures to grams (weight) or milliliters (volume).

STANDARD CUP	FINE POWDER (ex. flour)	GRAIN (ex. rice)	GRANULAR (ex. sugar)	LIQUID SOLIDS (ex. butter)	LIQUID (ex. milk)
1	140 g	150 g	190 g	200 g	240 ml
3/4	105 g	113 g	143 g	150 g	180 ml
2/3	93 g	100 g	125 g	133 g	160 ml
1/2	70 g	75 g	95 g	100 g	120 ml
1/3	47 g	50 g	63 g	67 g	80 ml
1/4	35 g	38 g	48 g	50 g	60 ml
1/8	18 g	19 g	24 g	25 g	30 ml

Useful Equivalents for Liquid Ingredients by Volume

TSP	TBSP	CUPS	FL OZ	ML	L
1/4 tsp				1 ml	
1/2 tsp				2 ml	
1 tsp				5 ml	
3 tsp	1 Tbsp		1/2 fl oz	15 ml	
	2 Tbsp	1/8 cup	1 fl oz	30 ml	
	4 Tbsp	1/4 cup	2 fl oz	60 ml	
	5 1/3 Tbsp	1/3 cup	3 fl oz	80 ml	
	8 Tbsp	1/2 cup	4 fl oz	120 ml	
	10 2/3 Tbsp	2/3 cup	5 fl oz	160 ml	
	12 Tbsp	3/4 cup	6 fl oz	180 ml	
	16 Tbsp	1 cup	8 fl oz	240 ml	
	1 pt	2 cups	16 fl oz	480 ml	
	1 qt	4 cups	32 fl oz	960 ml	
			33 fl oz	1000 ml	1 L

Useful Equivalents for Dry Ingredients by Weight

(To convert ounces to grams, multiply the number of ounces by 30.)

OZ	LB	G
1 oz	1/16 lb	30 g
4 oz	1/4 lb	120 g
8 oz	1/2 lb	240 g
12 oz	3/4 lb	360 g
16 oz	1 lb	480 g

Useful Equivalents for Length

(To convert inches to centimeters, multiply the number of inches by 2.5.)

IN	FT	YD	CM	M
1 in			2.5 cm	
6 in	1/2 ft		15 cm	
12 in	1 ft		30 cm	
36 in	3 ft	1 yd	90 cm	
40 in			100 cm	1 m

Useful Equivalents for Cooking/Oven Temperatures

	FAHRENHEIT	CELSIUS	GAS MARK
FREEZE WATER	32°F	0°C	
ROOM TEMPERATURE	68°F	20°C	
BOIL WATER	212°F	100°C	
	325°F	160°C	3
	350°F	180°C	4
	375°F	190°C	5
	400°F	200°C	6
	425°F	220°C	7
	450°F	230°C	8
BROIL			Grill

Recipe Index

DOTDASH MEREDITH CONSUMER MARKETING
Director, Direct Marketing-Books: Daniel Fagan
Marketing Operations Manager: Max Daily
Marketing Manager: Kylie Dazzo
Senior Marketing Coordinator: Elizabeth Moore
Content Manager: Julie Doll
Senior Production Manager: Liza Ward

PRODUCED BY:
BLUELINE CREATIVE GROUP LLC
visit: bluelinecreativegroup.com
Producer/Editor: Katherine Cobbs
Book Designer: Claire Cormany

LOCATION PHOTOGRAPHY:
Location Photographers: Emily Hart, Brandon Smith / Dwelling Table
Location Stylist: Sara Gae Waters

STUDIO PHOTOGRAPHY:
Photographer: Caitlin Bensel
Prop Stylist: Kay E. Clarke
Prop Styling Assistant: Caleb Clarke
Food Stylist: Torie Cox
Food Styling Assistants: Sally McKay, Carrie Marie Sawyer

PRINT PRODUCTION:
WATERBURY PUBLICATIONS, INC.

Library of Congress Control Number: 2024933923

ISBN-13: 978-1-4197-7937-4

First Edition 2024
Printed in the United States of America
10 9 8 7 6 5 4 3 2 1
Call 1-800-826-4707 for more information

Distributed in 2024 by Abrams, an imprint of ABRAMS.
Abrams® is a registered trademark of Harry N. Abrams, Inc.

ABRAMS The Art of Books
195 Broadway, New York, NY 10007
abramsbooks.com

HOLIDAY PLANNER

Simplify your holiday season and keep spirits bright with this helpful planner. Manage guest lists, keep tabs on gifts for family and friends, and stay on top of all your holiday to-dos for a low-stress holiday season.

November 2024 *daily to-dos:*

SUNDAY	MONDAY	TUESDAY	WEDNESDAY
Daylight saving time ends. Turn clocks back 1 hour at bedtime!	Get gift ideas from friends and family to get a jump start on holiday shopping.	Are you guest ready? Tidy up and tackle repairs around the home.	Take inventory. Buy or borrow any cookware or serving pieces needed.
3	**4**	**5**	**6**
Order holiday cards and update your address list (page 189).	It's Veterans Day. Take a break and remember our veterans.	Buy nonperishables like nuts and dried fruit in bulk to save.	Clean and organize the fridge.
10	**11**	**12**	**13**
Iron linens, polish the silver, wash glassware and dishes.	Make your game plan for Thanksgiving week.	Get fired up! Clean the fireplace and take stock of candles and votives.	Make a prep list for each dish.
17	**18**	**19**	**20**
Serving a frozen bird? Allow 1 day to thaw in the fridge for every 4 pounds.	Shop for perishable grocery items such as milk, cheese, and produce.	Buy fresh flowers and materials for your centerpieces (page 44).	Queue up some tunes, don your apron, and get a jump start on cooking.
24	**25**	**26**	**27**

THURSDAY	FRIDAY	SATURDAY
	Stock up on pumpkins for the Grateful Gathering centerpiece (page 58). …… …… …… **1**	Make your Thanksgiving guest list, menu plan, and shopping list. …… …… …… **2**
Set out the dishes you plan to use and label with what will go in each. …… …… …… **7**	Order your fresh bird now. …… …… …… **8**	Plan your centerpiece (page 44) and table setting. …… …… …… **9**
Plan your seating chart and make place cards. …… …… …… **14**	Tidy the least-used rooms in the house, which are less likely to get messy again. …… …… …… **15**	Round up board games, playing cards, and photo albums to entertain guests. …… …… …… **16**
Thanksgiving is a week away. Breathe and pamper yourself today. …… …… …… **21**	Throwing a Christmas party? Send invites now. Calendars fill fast! …… …… …… **22**	Need a kids' table? Wrap a small table with kraft paper and provide crayons. …… …… …… **23**
It's time for a Grateful Gathering (page 58). Happy Thanksgiving! …… …… …… **Thanksgiving 28**	It's Black Friday! Check your list twice. …… …… …… **29**	Enjoy those Thanksgiving leftovers! …… …… …… **30**

Marbleized Ornament
how—to:

Marbleize clear glass or plastic ornaments by removing the loop at the top and adding a few drops of acrylic paint in your chosen colors. Tip the ornaments from side to side to swirl the paint around the interior. Let the ornaments dry for a few days before replacing the top loops and adding ribbon or a hook for hanging.

HOLIDAY HOTLINES

Use these toll-free numbers when you have last-minute food questions.

USDA Meat & Poultry Hotline:
1-888-674-6854

FDA Center for Food Safety:
1-888-723-3366

Butterball Turkey Talk Line:
1-800-BUTTERBALL

Butterball Turkey Text Line:
1-844-877-3456

Jennie-O Turkey Hotline:
1-800-TURKEYS

Ocean Spray Holiday Helpline:
1-800-662-3263

Fleischmann's Yeast Baker
Hotline: 1-800-777-4959

December 2024 *daily to-dos:*

SUNDAY	MONDAY	TUESDAY	WEDNESDAY
Deck those halls! Visit the tree lot to pick your tree or unpack the faux fir. **1**	Online shoppers, start clicking! Cyber Monday is here. **2**	Test the Christmas lights and replace fuses or strands. **3**	Purchase stamps, gift wrap, tags, ribbons, tape, and scissors. **4**
Give back: Sign up to deliver meals or visit the sick or homebound. **8**	Dehydrate citrus slices for pretty ornaments. **9**	Fill bird feeders with seed for overwintering songbirds. **10**	Hang wreaths, dress the mantel, display cards, and show off Christmas accents for weeks of enjoyment. **11**
Finalize online purchases today before shipping prices soar. **15**	Show appreciation. Give teachers, mail carriers, and babysitters small gifts. **16**	Simmer spices and orange slices in water to add a festive aroma to your home. **17**	Watch a beloved holiday film by a roaring fire. **18**
Tidy up the house to let good tidings begin. **22**	Don't forget the stocking stuffers —and water that tree again! **23**	Welcome friends and family for Christmas Cheers! (page 72). **Christmas Eve 24**	Merry Christmas! Gather for a Classic Christmas Supper (page 90). **Christmas Day 25**
Return or exchange any gifts before return deadlines. **29**	Get a jump start on those thank-you notes. **30**	Raise a glass and usher in 2025! **New Year's Eve 31**	

THURSDAY	FRIDAY	SATURDAY
Make cookie dough and freeze, or bake cookies and cakes and freeze unfrosted.	Send those holiday cards. Don't wait until post office lines grow.	Check expiration dates on unused gift cards and use them to buy gifts for others.
....	....	....
....	....	....
....	....	....
5	**6**	**7**
Water that fresh Christmas tree!	Bake It Forward! (page 156) with gifts from the kitchen for friends and colleagues.	Get tickets to holiday performances.
....	....	....
....	....	....
....	....	....
12	**13**	**14**
Practice self-care. Enjoy a hot bath, coffee with a pal, or a winter's nap.	Invite friends for a casual Feel-Good Feast (page 82).	Hello, first day of winter! Bundle up for caroling or enjoy the Christmas lights.
....	....	....
....	....	....
....	....	....
19	**20**	**Winter Solstice 21**
Go for a family walk, bike, or hike.	Plan your goals, intentions, or resolutions for the year ahead.	Phone loved ones you missed this holiday.
....	....	....
....	....	....
....	....	....
Boxing Day 26	**27**	**28**

Block-Print Wrapping Paper
how-to:

A carved wooden stamp, foam roller or brush, acrylic paint, and some solid matte wrapping paper are all you need to make your own block-print wrapping paper. Find batik and botanical wooden stamps on Etsy, or buy a complete block-printing kit online from Molly Mahon.

....
....
....
....
....
....
....
....
....
....
....

Decorating Planner

Here's a list of details and finishing touches you can use to
tailor a picture-perfect house this holiday season.

Decorative materials needed

FROM THE YARD ....

FROM AROUND THE HOUSE ....
....

FROM THE STORE..
....

OTHER..

Holiday decorations

FOR THE TABLE ....
....

FOR THE DOOR..
....

FOR THE MANTEL...
....

FOR THE STAIRCASE ....
....

OTHER..

Create a Decorator's Toolkit

Our photo stylists guard their toolkits like the family jewels. A well-stocked kit means
you have just what you need at the ready to get you through the holidays and beyond.

- ☐ Tools (hammer, screwdrivers, clamps)
- ☐ Nails, screws, S-hooks, tacks
- ☐ Adhesive strips and hooks
- ☐ Staple gun and staples
- ☐ Hot-glue gun and glue sticks
- ☐ Crafts glue
- ☐ Super-glue
- ☐ Clothespins
- ☐ Funnel
- ☐ Tape measure
- ☐ Twine

- ☐ Fishing line
- ☐ Green florists wire
- ☐ Sewing kit
- ☐ Lint roller
- ☐ Steamer or iron
- ☐ Paintbrushes (assorted)
- ☐ Scissors
- ☐ Florists snips
- ☐ Lighter
- ☐ Batteries (assorted)
- ☐ Fuses for Christmas lights
- ☐ Clear tape

- ☐ Double-sided tape
- ☐ Painters tape
- ☐ Museum Wax
- ☐ Putty
- ☐ Goo-gone
- ☐ WD-40
- ☐ Window cleaner
- ☐ Furniture polish
- ☐ Touch-up paint
- ☐ Static duster
- ☐ Stain stick

How Lovely Are Your Branches!

EIGHT TYPES OF GREENERY FOR LUSH GARLANDS

 SILVER DOLLAR AND SEEDED EUCALYPTUS are fragrant choices with striking blue-gray leaves and tight berries that look more loose and modern than the usual conifers. Eucalyptus is great for flower arrangements because it has a long life when kept in a vase of water. It has a pleasing scent too.

 CEDAR'S natural oils and striking leaf edges give branches staying power. With its dramatic draping effect, cedar looks great just about anywhere you choose to weave it in. Its lovely smell keeps moths at bay to boot.

 BOXWOOD boasts tiny, roundish green leaves and a tight form that stays fresh-looking for weeks. Use it to adorn staircases, frame entryways, make wreaths, and more. It's a material that adds elegance to any holiday decor.

 JUNIPER delivers fragrance, striking blue berries, and hardy leaves that hold up well whether used inside or out. Wear garden gloves when working with juniper to protect hands from its prickly foliage.

 **OLIVE** branches lend a modern Mediterranean feel to arrangements with foliage that curls as it dries for an interesting effect. Mist it regularly with water if to keep it looking fresh.

 **FIR** branches are a gorgeous deep green with a dense habit that's a beloved holiday classic material for centerpieces, mantels, mailboxes, and swags for sconces or doors.

 PINE has long, silky green needles and a refreshing, clean scent. It adds a gorgeous contrasting texture when tucked into floral arrangements and mixed evergreen wreaths.

 **MAGNOLIA** boasts big, sturdy, glossy-green leaves with velvety copper backs that lend a striking, natural palette to holiday decorating. If stored in a cool, dry place, magnolia wreaths and garlands can last for years.

Party Planner

Stay on top of your party plans with this time-saving menu organizer.

GUESTS	WHAT THEY'RE BRINGING	SERVING PIECES NEEDED
....	☐ appetizer ☐ beverage ☐ bread ☐ main dish ☐ side dish ☐ dessert	....
....	☐ appetizer ☐ beverage ☐ bread ☐ main dish ☐ side dish ☐ dessert	....
....	☐ appetizer ☐ beverage ☐ bread ☐ main dish ☐ side dish ☐ dessert	....
....	☐ appetizer ☐ beverage ☐ bread ☐ main dish ☐ side dish ☐ dessert	....
....	☐ appetizer ☐ beverage ☐ bread ☐ main dish ☐ side dish ☐ dessert	....
....	☐ appetizer ☐ beverage ☐ bread ☐ main dish ☐ side dish ☐ dessert	....
....	☐ appetizer ☐ beverage ☐ bread ☐ main dish ☐ side dish ☐ dessert	....
....	☐ appetizer ☐ beverage ☐ bread ☐ main dish ☐ side dish ☐ dessert	....
....	☐ appetizer ☐ beverage ☐ bread ☐ main dish ☐ side dish ☐ dessert	....
....	☐ appetizer ☐ beverage ☐ bread ☐ main dish ☐ side dish ☐ dessert	....
....	☐ appetizer ☐ beverage ☐ bread ☐ main dish ☐ side dish ☐ dessert	....
....	☐ appetizer ☐ beverage ☐ bread ☐ main dish ☐ side dish ☐ dessert	....
....	☐ appetizer ☐ beverage ☐ bread ☐ main dish ☐ side dish ☐ dessert	....
....	☐ appetizer ☐ beverage ☐ bread ☐ main dish ☐ side dish ☐ dessert	....
....	☐ appetizer ☐ beverage ☐ bread ☐ main dish ☐ side dish ☐ dessert	....
....	☐ appetizer ☐ beverage ☐ bread ☐ main dish ☐ side dish ☐ dessert	....
....	☐ appetizer ☐ beverage ☐ bread ☐ main dish ☐ side dish ☐ dessert	....

Party Guest List

Party To-Do List

Christmas Dinner Planner

Use this space to create a menu, to-do list, and guest list for your special holiday celebration.

Menu Ideas

....
....
....
....
....
....
....

Dinner To-Do List

....
....
....
....
....
....
....

Christmas Dinner Guest List

....
....
....
....
....
....
....
....
....

Pantry List

....
....
....
....
....
....
....
....
....
....
....
....
....
....
....
....
....
....
....
....
....
....
....
....
....
....
....
....

Grocery List

....
....
....
....
....
....
....
....
....
....
....
....
....
....
....
....
....
....
....
....
....
....
....
....
....
....
....
....

Gifts & Greetings

Keep up with family and friends' sizes, jot down gift ideas, and record purchases in this convenient chart. Also, use it to keep track of addresses for your Christmas card list.

Gift List and Size Charts

	GIFT PURCHASED/MADE	SENT
jeans_____ shirt_____ sweater_____ jacket_____ shoes_____ belt_____ blouse_____ skirt_____ slacks_____ dress_____ suit_____ coat_____ pajamas_____ robe_____ hat_____ gloves_____ ring_____		
jeans_____ shirt_____ sweater_____ jacket_____ shoes_____ belt_____ blouse_____ skirt_____ slacks_____ dress_____ suit_____ coat_____ pajamas_____ robe_____ hat_____ gloves_____ ring_____		
jeans_____ shirt_____ sweater_____ jacket_____ shoes_____ belt_____ blouse_____ skirt_____ slacks_____ dress_____ suit_____ coat_____ pajamas_____ robe_____ hat_____ gloves_____ ring_____		
jeans_____ shirt_____ sweater_____ jacket_____ shoes_____ belt_____ blouse_____ skirt_____ slacks_____ dress_____ suit_____ coat_____ pajamas_____ robe_____ hat_____ gloves_____ ring_____		
jeans_____ shirt_____ sweater_____ jacket_____ shoes_____ belt_____ blouse_____ skirt_____ slacks_____ dress_____ suit_____ coat_____ pajamas_____ robe_____ hat_____ gloves_____ ring_____		
jeans_____ shirt_____ sweater_____ jacket_____ shoes_____ belt_____ blouse_____ skirt_____ slacks_____ dress_____ suit_____ coat_____ pajamas_____ robe_____ hat_____ gloves_____ ring_____		
jeans_____ shirt_____ sweater_____ jacket_____ shoes_____ belt_____ blouse_____ skirt_____ slacks_____ dress_____ suit_____ coat_____ pajamas_____ robe_____ hat_____ gloves_____ ring_____		

Christmas Card List

NAME	ADDRESS	SENT

Holiday Memories

Hold on to priceless Christmas memories forever with handwritten
recollections of this season's magical moments.

Treasured Traditions

Keep track of your family's favorite holiday customs and pastimes on these lines.

....

....

....

....

....

....

....

....

....

....

....

Special Holiday Activities

What holiday events do you look forward to year after year? Write them down here.

....

....

....

....

....

....

....

....

....

....

Holiday Visits and Visitors

Keep a list of this year's holiday visitors.
Jot down friend and family news as well.

....
....
....
....
....
....
....
....
....
....
....
....
....
....
....
....
....
....
....
....
....
....
....
....
....
....
....

This Year's Favorite Recipes

APPETIZERS AND BEVERAGES

....
....
....
....
....

ENTRÉES ....

....
....
....
....

SIDES AND SALADS ....

....
....
....

COOKIES AND CANDIES ....

....
....
....
....

DESSERTS ....

....
....
....

Looking Ahead

Holiday Wrap-Up

Use this checklist to record thank-you notes sent for holiday gifts and hospitality.

NAME	GIFT AND/OR EVENT	NOTE SENT
....	....	☐
....	....	☐
....	....	☐
....	....	☐
....	....	☐
....	....	☐
....	....	☐
....	....	☐
....	....	☐
....	....	☐
....	....	☐
....	....	☐

Notes for Next Year

Write down your ideas for Christmas 2025 on the lines below.

....

....

....

....

....

....

....

In memory of Charlie